Welcome to the course

Welcome to Modern World History! Studying this subject will help you to understand the world you live in: the events of the last century can help to explain the problems and opportunities that exist in the world today.

There are four units in the course and each is worth 25% of the whole GCSE. Those units are:

- **Unit 1** International Relations: The Era of the Cold War 1943–91
- **Unit 2** Modern World Depth Study (Germany 1918–39; Russia 1914–39; or USA 1919–41)
- **Unit 3** Modern World Source Enquiry (War and the transformation of British society 1903–28; War and the transformation of British Society 1931–51; or The transformation of British society 1951–79)
- **Unit 4** Representations of History (your controlled assessment task).

Key terms are emboldened in the text, and definitions can be found in the glossary.

We've broken down the six stages of revision to ensure you are prepared every step of the way.

Zone in: how to get into the perfect 'zone' for revision.

Planning zone: tips and advice on how to plan revision effectively.

Know zone: the facts you need to know, memory tips and exam-style practice for every section.

Don't panic zone: last-minute revision tips.

Exam zone: what to expect on the exam paper.

Zone out: what happens after the exams.

There are also Examzone features throughout the text to help you understand how to improve, with guidance on answering exam-style questions, tips on how to remember important concepts and how to avoid common pitfalls.

There are three different types of feature throughout this book:

Top Tips provide handy hints on how to apply what you have learned and how to remember key information and concepts.

> **exam zone**
> **Top tip**
>
> The sources in this book contain evidence of how people thought about the Cold War at the time. You do not have to memorise these sources. However, if you can summarise their information in one sentence you may be able to use this in the exam.

> **exam zone**
> **Watch out!**
>
> Do not confuse Cominform with Comecon. Remember Comecon is economic, and Cominform is political.

Watch out! These warn you about common mistakes and misconceptions that are often made.

Build better answers give you an opportunity to answer exam-style questions. They include tips for what a basic ■, good ● and excellent △ answer will contain.

> **exam zone**
> **Build better answers**
>
> Exam question: Describe the key features of Cominform. (6 marks)
> You need to make developed statements that answer the question and describe why the features mentioned in the answer are important.
>
> ■ A basic answer (level 1): One key feature of Cominform was that it allowed Stalin to control Eastern Europe.
>
> ● A good answer (level 2): One key feature of Cominform was that it allowed Stalin to control Eastern Europe. At Cominform's first conference, leaders of Eastern European countries agreed with Stalin to boycott Marshall Aid.
>
> △ An excellent answer (full marks) fully describes two or three key features.

The Know Zone Build better answers pages at the end of this book include an exam-style question, tips on how to approach the question, a student answer and an improved student answer so that you can see how to improve your own writing.

Key Topic I: How did the Cold War in Europe develop? 1943–56

How many world wars have there been? This seems like an easy question. There were two – the first between 1914 and 1918, and the second between 1939 and 1945. However, some American writers have suggested that there was a Third World War, between Russia and America, which started in 1945 and ended in 1991 with the fall of the Soviet Union. This war is better known as the Cold War.

In this section you will study:

- why the Cold War began: the widening gulf between the USA and the USSR and the development of the Iron Curtain
- the development of the Cold War in Europe: dividing Germany and Europe, 1947–55
- Hungary under Soviet rule, 1949–56.

You will consider the breakdown in trust between the USSR (the Union of Soviet Socialist Republics, also known as the Soviet Union or by its old name, Russia) and America following their victory in the Second World War, and how this led to a division of Europe. Additionally, you will see how ideology, the attitudes and personalities of powerful men, and the development of the atom bomb intensified conflict in the late 1940s. Finally, you will consider two flashpoints of the Cold War: Berlin and Hungary.

What was the Cold War?

Can we really call the Cold War the Third World War? There were important differences between the First World War and the Second World War on the one hand, and the Cold War on the other. The Cold War was a new kind of conflict in which America and the USSR never declared war on each other, nor did American and Soviet soldiers face each other in battle. In fact, during much of the time there was a 'Cold Peace' – a stand-off between the USSR and America – because both sides knew that a real Third World War, a nuclear war, would be unwinnable.

However, although the USSR and America never fought each other, the Cold War had many of the characteristics of an actual war. For example, both sides were involved in an **arms race**, a military build-up of nuclear weapons as well as armies, navies and air forces. Both sides formed military **alliances** and were involved in spying on each other. Each side was committed to a different set of ideas or ideology. Finally, **propaganda** was an essential aspect of the Cold War. Governments used propaganda to persuade their own citizens that they were under threat and therefore that the military build-up was necessary. Propaganda was also essential to show why enemies were evil and why they needed to be fought.

*A thermonuclear test explosion in 1954. The USSR and America never used atomic weapons against each other, however, the development of arms and fear of a **nuclear holocaust** characterised the Cold War period.*

Why did the Cold War begin? The breakdown of the Grand Alliance

Learning objectives

In this chapter you will learn about:

- the difference between communism and capitalism
- the three key meetings of the Grand Alliance
- the difficult relationship between Russia and America.

The Grand Alliance (1941)

Prior to the Cold War, America and the USSR worked together as members of the **Grand Alliance**: an alliance created in 1941 to defeat the Nazis. However, the Grand Alliance was a marriage of convenience between communists and capitalists united only in their opposition to Hitler. Once Hitler had been defeated, the Alliance became increasingly uneasy. Between 1943 and 1945, the leaders of the Grand Alliance met at three international conferences: Teheran, Yalta and Potsdam.

	Capitalism	**Communism**
Focus	Individual rights	The rights of the working class
Values	Individual freedom	Equality
Economy:	Free trade	Government planned
Politics	Democratic elections	Communist Party controls government

The leaders each wanted the others to recognise that there were countries that fell within their 'sphere of influence' and countries that did not. None of the official documents that were signed laid out these spheres. Nevertheless, by the end of the three conferences, it was clear that there was broad agreement over what these were.

- The USSR would 'influence' Poland, Czechoslovakia, the Baltic States, Hungary and Romania. This would build a line of 'buffer states' between the USSR and the West. Stalin agreed this could be 'influence' only, with these states having free elections and a level of democracy (this was built into the document signed at Yalta).
- The USSR also wanted its influence in Yugoslavia (which had its own communist government) accepted. Yugoslavia was officially accepted as a communist country at Yalta.

- Britain and the USA were keen to get the USSR to accept their influence in Western Europe, Greece and Italy.

The Teheran Conference (1943)

When Churchill, Stalin and Roosevelt met at Teheran (28 November–1 December 1943), they reached some definite agreements and some agreements in principle (without outlining the detail). Stalin was annoyed that Britain and the USA had delayed opening a second front in the war. He was convinced they were waiting for the communist USSR to damage itself fatally in the battle against Nazi Germany before they would intervene.

- The USA and Britain would open a second front to split the German defences and take some of the pressure off the USSR. Stalin had been urging them to do this for some time, while Britain and the USA had wanted to focus on a single front. However, Roosevelt supported the second front idea and it was agreed to start in June 1944.
- The USSR would declare war on Japan once Germany was defeated.
- Poland should be given more land from Germany, but lose some to the USSR.

But there were points of disagreement, over which Roosevelt often sided with Stalin, not Churchill. For example, Churchill wanted to begin an invasion of the Balkans. While this would help the war effort, he mainly wanted it to stop the Soviet advance in Eastern Europe (and via this the spread of communism).

Why did the Cold War begin? The breakdown of the Grand Alliance

7

Not surprisingly, Stalin opposed this and Roosevelt supported Stalin. He favoured the second front in the west proposed by Stalin and an invasion of the Balkans as well would have weakened the Allied forces by splitting them up too much.

The Yalta Conference (1945)

When Churchill, Stalin and Roosevelt met at Yalta (4–11 February 1945), they agreed on some of the same things they had agreed at Teheran, but with some changes.

- Germany, when defeated, would be reduced in size, would be demilitarised and would have to pay reparations (these would be taken in materials, goods and labour).
- Plans were begun for how Germany would be divided after the war. The rebuilding of Europe was to be done along the lines of the Atlantic Charter agreed between the USA and Britain in 1941, the most important policy of which was the right of countries to choose their own governments.
- The Nazi Party would be banned and war criminals tried in front of an international court.
- A United Nations Organisation (UN) would be set up to replace the League of Nations. It would meet for the first time on 25 April 1945. It was decided who would be members: all the Allies and those who had agreed to join the UN on 8 February 1945. The Soviet Republics of Ukraine and Belorussia were to be seen as separate countries from the USSR and to have their own voting rights. The USA would draw up the Charter.
- The USSR would declare war on Japan three months after the defeat of Germany. There was an outline of how lands held by Japan would be divided after the war (the USSR would have land Japan had captured returned).
- Poland (at present communist, under Soviet control) should be in the Soviet 'sphere of influence' but be run on 'a broader democratic basis'.

The conference was a success largely because of the understanding between Stalin and Roosevelt, established at Teheran in 1943. Roosevelt also worked well with Churchill. However, splits were growing. Britain and the USA had been reluctant to agree to Poland becoming communist.

Britain had entered the Second World War to defend Poland, while America wished to avoid communism spreading further west and antagonising the many Americans who had Polish roots. Stalin, on the other hand, desperately wanted Poland as a buffer between the USSR and the West. The USSR had been invaded from the West no less than three times already that century.

Signs of tension

In spite of the apparent unity, there were important issues that divided the '**Big Three**' – Stalin, Roosevelt and Churchill. For example, although they all agreed to work for democracy, there were significant disagreements over what democracy meant.

Stalin believed that a democratic government had to be a communist government because only the communists truly represented the working people. Roosevelt, on the other hand, believed that democracy involved a number of different political parties competing to win the people's support in free elections.

The success of the conference was based largely on Stalin's relationship with Roosevelt. However, within two months Roosevelt had died and the new American President, Harry S. Truman, was less willing to compromise with Stalin. This led to further tensions at the Alliance's final conference.

The 'Big Three' at the Yalta Conference, February 1945. From left to right: Churchill, Roosevelt, Stalin.

The Potsdam Conference (1945)

When Churchill, Stalin and Truman met at Potsdam (July and August 1945), there was far more tension. President Truman had been briefed about the earlier conferences. But he had no relationship with Stalin. To add to the disruption, the result of the British election came during the conference, and the new Labour Prime Minster, Attlee, replaced Churchill.

So the personal trust and understanding built up in earlier conferences was lost. Truman had delayed the first meeting of the conference until after the new **atomic bomb** had been tested. The fact that Stalin had been told nothing of the bomb until this point increased his suspicion of his allies. Also, Germany was defeated, so the Big Three were no longer united by a common enemy.

Despite this, they reached agreement on many points concerning the reconstruction of Europe. It went into great detail about the terms as they applied to Germany – from how reparations were to be paid to how the military equipment was to be broken up. They agreed to:

- set up a Council of Foreign Ministers to organise the re-building of Europe.
- ban the Nazi Party and prosecute surviving Nazis as war criminals in a special court run by the Allies at Nuremberg
- reduce the size of Germany
- divide Germany into four zones, to be administered by the USA, the USSR, Britain and France, with the aim of re-uniting it under one government as soon as possible
- divide Berlin, Germany's capital, into four as well, despite it being deep in the USSR's zone
- give the USSR a quarter of the industrial equipment from the other three zones, because its zone was the least developed industrially, but had to provide the other zones with raw materials such as coal.

Once again, however, there was disagreement on bigger issues.

Reparations

The USSR wanted to impose heavy reparations on Germany, whereas America wanted Germany to be rebuilt. The Conference agreed a compromise whereby each ally would take reparations from the zone they occupied. This was far less than Stalin wanted, as the part of Germany that he controlled was poorer than the rest and had much less industry. As a result, the Western Allies agreed to hand over industrial equipment in exchange for raw materials.

The atomic bomb

Truman attempted to assert his authority during the Potsdam Conference. He believed that America possessed the ultimate weapon in the atomic bomb and therefore, in Churchill's words, 'generally bossed the whole meeting'. Truman believed that the atomic bomb was 'the master card' in the Potsdam discussions. It gave America the power to destroy entire enemy cities without risking a single American life.

Stalin refused to be pushed around. Truman later remarked that when Stalin was informed about the bomb he 'showed no special interest'. However, Stalin was well aware of the significance of the atomic bomb and had, as early as 1940, instructed Soviet scientists to develop their own. News of the American bomb made Stalin more determined than ever to protect the interests of the USSR. Stalin's plan was to protect the USSR by creating a 'buffer zone' – a communist area in Eastern Europe between the USSR and the capitalist west.

Poland

Truman's arrogance and Stalin's determination soured the relationship at the centre of the Grand Alliance. Their relationship was further strained by the USSR's actions in Poland. Stalin had agreed to set up a government in Poland that included both communists and capitalists. However, by the time of the Potsdam Conference it was evident that he had broken his word.

Exam-style question

Explain the importance of three of the following in international relations.
- **The Teheran Conference, 1943**
- **The Yalta Conference, 1945**
- **The Potsdam Conference, 1945**
- **The development of the atomic bomb**   **(15 marks)**

Why did the Cold War begin? The breakdown of the Grand Alliance

9

Although the Potsdam Conference finished with a show of unity, insiders at the conference were aware that there were bitter divisions between America and the USSR, which some thought would lead to a new war.

Greece

An early battleground for these tensions was found in Greece. The German retreat in 1944 left two groups fighting to rule the country: monarchists and communists. In 1945 British troops were sent in to support the monarchists under the claim of restoring order and supervising free elections. The USSR complained to the United Nations and a civil war erupted. When the British decided to pull out, in 1947, the US stepped in to prop up the king's government.

Activities

1 Divide the following conference aims into those belonging to the USA, those belonging to the USSR, and those shared by both:

- a 'sphere of influence' in Eastern Europe
- reparations from Germany
- governments representing working people
- a peaceful and prosperous Germany
- governments elected by the people
- prosecution of Nazi war criminals
- a communist government in Poland
- democratic governments across Europe.

2 The three conferences – Teheran, Yalta and Potsdam – form the background to the Cold War. During this period it became clear that relations between the USSR and America were uneasy. This activity will help you to understand how these relationships developed.

- On a large piece of paper, draw the following axes:

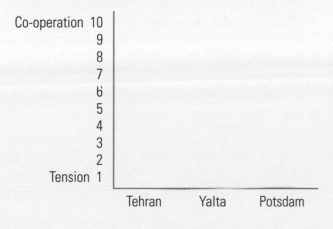

- For each conference, make two lists: a) evidence that the 'Big Three' were co-operating, and b) evidence that there was tension in their relationship.

- Use the information on your lists to reach a judgment about the extent to which the 'Big Three' were co-operating at each conference. Give the 'Big Three' a mark out of 10, where 10 represents complete co-operation and 1 represents great tension.

- Plot the scores for each conference on your graph.

- In what ways did the relationship between the 'Big Three' change during this period?

- Make a list of reasons why the relationship between the 'Big Three' changed between the Teheran Conference in 1943 and the Potsdam Conference in 1945.

Why did the Cold War begin? Fear of war

> ### Learning objectives
>
> In this chapter you will learn about:
> - the breakdown of trust between Russia and America
> - how Russia and America viewed each other in 1946.

The war of words

During 1946 it became increasingly clear that Europe had been divided between capitalism in the west and communism in the east. Stalin, representing the East, and Churchill, representing the West (despite no longer being Britain's leader), responded with a 'war of words', showing that the former allies now viewed each other with tremendous suspicion. This suspicion became an important part of the Cold War.

> From Stettin in the Baltic to Trieste in the Adriatic, an iron curtain has descended across the continent. Behind the line lie all the capitals of the ancient states of Central and Eastern Europe… all these famous cities and the populations around them lie in the Soviet sphere and all are subject, in one form or another, not only to Soviet influence but to a very high and increasing measure of control from Moscow.

Source A: Churchill's 'Iron Curtain' speech, March 1946

> Essentially, Mr Churchill now adopts the position of the warmonger, and in this Mr Churchill is not alone. He has friends not only in Britain but in the United States of America as well. A point to be noted in this respect is that Mr Churchill and his friends bear a striking resemblance to Hitler and his friends.

Source B: Stalin's response to Churchill's speech, March 1946

Churchill gave his speech during a trip to America, and everyone understood that President Truman supported what he had said. Clearly, both sides had started to view each other as opponents rather than allies.

Secret telegrams

Truman and Stalin were concerned about the breakdown of the Grand Alliance and the threat of a new war. Both men asked for secret reports from their embassies to help them to understand how their opponents were thinking. Both reports were sent as telegrams.

The Long Telegram (1946)

Truman received worrying news in the 'Long Telegram', a secret report from Kennan, America's ambassador in Moscow. The telegram reported that:

- Stalin had given a speech calling for the destruction of capitalism
- there could be no peace with the USSR while it was opposed to capitalism
- the USSR was building up its military power.
- the USA should seek to contain communism.

Novikov's Telegram (1946)

Novikov, the Soviet ambassador to America, sent a telegram to Stalin which was equally concerning. It reported:

- America desired to dominate the world
- following Roosevelt's death, the American government was no longer interested in co-operation with the USSR
- the American public was being prepared for war with the USSR.

Following these secret telegrams, both governments believed that they were facing the possibility of war. Indeed, the government of the USSR came to believe that war with America was inevitable. In America, some soldiers who had fought in the Second World War and entered politics when they returned home called Stalin 'the new Hitler'. Their point was simple: Stalin, like Hitler, was preparing for war and must be stopped.

On the verge of the Cold War

By the end of 1946, the Grand Alliance was all but over. America had come to believe that the USSR was planning world domination and many in the USSR feared that America was planning the same. At the beginning of 1947, Truman addressed the American government, setting out his belief that America must stand against communism. This speech, setting out the 'Truman **Doctrine**', can be seen as the unofficial declaration of the Cold War. You will read more about the Truman Doctrine on page 12.

President Truman making the Truman Doctrine speech in March 1947.

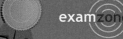

examzone
Top tip

The sources in this book contain evidence of how people thought about the Cold War at the time. You do not have to memorise these sources. However, if you can summarise their information in one sentence you may be able to use this in the exam.

examzone
Build better answers

Exam Question: Give two reasons from Source A that explain why Winston Churchill believed that the Soviet Union had divided Europe. (2 marks)

■ **A basic answer** identifies one reason.

● **A good answer** identifies two reasons.

Look at the question above and read Source A. Use the information in the source to provide a good answer to the question.

Activities

1 Divide your class into three teams. Each team must prepare a short speech explaining who they believe was responsible for the breakdown of the Grand Alliance.
   Team 1 will argue that the USA was to blame.
   Team 2 will argue that the USSR was to blame.
   Team 3 will argue that both sides share the blame.

2 Present your speeches in turn. Your teacher will award marks in the following way:
   • relevant and accurate statement – 1 point
   • specific supporting detail – 2 points
   • clear explanation of why the opposing side is to blame – 3 points.

   The team with the most points wins!

examzone
Watch out!

Do not confuse Churchill's 'Iron Curtain' with the Berlin Wall! The 'Iron Curtain' is a metaphor for the division of Europe, whereas the Berlin Wall was an actual barrier, put up in 1961, that divided Berlin (see pages 30–31).

The development of the Cold War: the Truman Doctrine and Marshall Aid

Learning objectives

In this chapter you will learn about:

- the key features of the Truman Doctrine and Marshall Aid
- America's reasons for offering Marshall Aid.

The Truman Doctrine (1947)

Following the 'Long Telegram' (see page 10), Truman asked the American military to assess the strength of the USSR's army. He learned that the USSR was in no position to wage a war. Nonetheless, Truman believed that the USSR had a second strategy that would allow it to conquer more and more territory without having to declare war: Stalin would encourage communist revolutions across Europe. After the Second World War, much of Europe was devastated and citizens in countries such as Italy, France, Greece, Turkey and the United Kingdom were suffering great hardships. In these conditions communism was highly appealing because communists believed that the wealth of the richest people should be shared out among the poor. To address this threat, in 1947 Truman set out a new policy that soon became known as the 'Truman Doctrine'.

The Truman Doctrine stated that:

- the world had a choice between communist tyranny and democratic freedom
- America had a responsibility to fight for liberty wherever it was threatened
- America would send troops and economic resources to help governments that were threatened by communists
- communism should not be allowed to grow and gain territory.

The significance of the Truman Doctrine

The Truman Doctrine was important because it suggested that America, rather than the United Nations, had a responsibility to protect the world. This marked a reversal of the USA's traditional policy of 'isolationism' by which America had stayed out of international affairs. It was also significant because it divided the world according to ideology: it stated clearly that capitalism and communism were in opposition.

This suggested that there could be no further co-operation between East and West due to their ideological differences, and in this sense it marked the unofficial end of the Grand Alliance and the beginning of the Cold War. Finally, it set a realistic goal for American foreign policy: Truman was committed to 'containment'. This implied that although America would not invade the USSR, it would make every effort to stop the spread of communism.

The Marshall Plan (1947)

Truman described containment and the Marshall Plan as 'two halves of the same walnut'. By this he meant that America had a dual strategy for dealing with communism. First, containment aimed to beat communism through military force. Secondly, the Marshall Plan of 1947 committed $13 billion of American money to rebuild the shattered economies of Europe. By encouraging prosperity, the Marshall Plan would weaken the attraction of communism. To those suffering economic hardship following the Second World War, the promise of sharing resources equally under communism had great appeal. If people were wealthy, however, the idea of sharing resources would have less appeal. In order to qualify for American money, European countries had to agree to trade freely with America. In this way, the Marshall Plan also helped the American economy.

Did you know?

The United Nations (UN) is an organisation created in 1945 to maintain international peace. The first meeting of the UN, in 1946, was attended by 51 nations. Today, the UN is made up of 192 nations.

Initial reaction to the Marshall Plan

European leaders met at the Paris Conference of 1948 to discuss the American offer. Many European countries were keen to receive Marshall Aid. However, representatives from the USSR walked out of the conference claiming that the Americans were attempting to split Europe into 'two camps'. They argued that Marshall Aid was the first step in creating a military alliance that would wage war on the Soviet Union. Stalin also insisted that Eastern European countries in the Soviet 'sphere of influence' refuse the help offered by America. By contrast, 16 countries including Britain and France welcomed the offer, seeing it as a way of rebuilding their economies and defeating communism in their own countries.

A British newspaper cartoon from June 1948 showing the 'Iron Curtain' and Marshall Aid. The figure on the right is Stalin. The figure looking over the 'Iron Curtain' is Tito, the communist leader of Yugoslavia. Although Tito was a communist, he did not see eye-to-eye with Stalin and found some aspects of Western Europe very attractive.

Activity

You are one of Truman's advisers. Prepare a letter to be sent to the leaders of all European governments inviting them to the Paris Conference of 1948. The letter should:

- describe America's offer of assistance (the Marshall Plan)
- explain why America is offering this assistance
- set out what governments must do in order to qualify for this offer.

Remember to be persuasive!

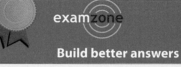

Build better answers

Exam question: Describe the key features of the Truman Doctrine.
(6 marks)

You need to identify important points, not simply write all you know. Here, for example, you could choose to describe an aim and an effect of the Truman Doctrine and a key point from what Truman said.

■ **A basic answer (level 1)** gives simple statements that are accurate but contain no supporting details.

● **A good answer (level 2)** gives a statement that is accurate and is developed with specific information.

▲ **An excellent answer (full marks)** contains two or three statements. Each statement explains a relevant key feature and is backed up with specific information.

For the exam question above, develop the following key features of the Truman Doctrine:
- containment
- the division of the world into two rival ideologies
- America has a responsibility to protect the world.

The development of the Cold War: satellite states

> ## Learning objectives
>
> In this chapter you will learn about:
> - the setting up of satellite states
> - why Stalin established Cominform and Comecon
> - how the 'spheres of influence' became 'two camps'.

What is a satellite state?

A satellite state is a country that is officially independent, but is in reality controlled by another country. Between 1947 and 1949, the USSR extended its influence over Eastern Europe, turning countries such as Czechoslovakia, Hungary and Poland into satellite states.

Why did Stalin set up satellite states?

Stalin described the Marshall Plan as 'dollar imperialism': he believed that the Americans were trying to buy influence over Europe, as any country that accepted Marshall Aid would effectively become an American ally. To prevent this, Stalin extended his control over Eastern Europe, creating a series of satellite states.

How did Stalin take control of them?

This emerged from the 'spheres of influence' discussed at the Teheran, Yalta and Potsdam conferences. At Yalta and Potsdam, the USSR agreed to free elections in these countries. It hoped at first that people would naturally choose communism in the free elections that the West wanted them to have. Some did, but most did not. So the USSR pushed for new 'free' elections that they fixed as much as they could. Once in power, they got rid of opposition parties and made each country a single-party state.

The USSR kept control by:

- making sure the Communist Party in each state had leaders that would obey Moscow
- creating an atmosphere of fear and mistrust so that it was difficult for people who wanted to oppose Soviet rule to trust each other enough to work together
- ruthlessly using the police and army in these states to stamp on any kind of opposition
- arranging the economies of these countries so that they were dependent on the USSR by 'rationalising' industries to stop the satellites being self-sufficient (e.g. Poland did all the shipbuilding, Hungary produced all the trucks).

ESTONIA

BALTIC STATES

LATVIA

LITHUANIA

Berlin●

EAST GERMANY

POLAND

SOVIET UNION

CZECHOSLOVAKIA

AUSTRIA

HUNGARY

ROMANIA

YUGOSLAVIA

BULGARIA

ALBANIA

GREECE

TURKEY

N

400 km

Land taken by USSR at the end of Second World War
Soviet-controlled communist countries
Non Soviet-controlled communist countries

Soviet expansion, 1945-48.

Yugoslavia

Communists, led by Marshal Tito, took over Yugoslavia in 1945, while the war was still going on. At first, Tito worked well with the USSR, but he wanted to run Yugoslavia himself, not follow orders as a satellite state. Relations worsened and Tito split from the USSR in 1948. He even took aid under the Marshall Plan.

Albania

Communists took over in Albania in 1945, while the war was still going on. It had the least opposition to becoming a satellite state.

The Baltic States

Estonia, Latvia and Lithuania became part of the Soviet Union after the war, as did what had been eastern Poland and part of Romania. There was no pretence of them being separate from the USSR, as there was with the satellite states. They were treated as part of the USSR.

East Germany

East Germany was the part of Germany that the USSR was given to administer when Germany was divided into zones at the end of the war. In 1949, after supposedly 'free' elections, it announced it was a separate country from the other three, Western-controlled, zones. It became the communist German Democratic Republic. In June 1953, demonstrations broke out across East Germany against communist policies, but the protests were crushed by Soviet tanks. Thousands were arrested and hundreds wounded.

Bulgaria

Late in 1944, while the war was still going on, a coalition of left-wing parties, including communists, took over in Bulgaria. In November 1945, they held 'free' elections which the communists won by intimidation. They then abolished all other political parties and executed anyone who looked able to oppose them, including many non-communists who had managed to get elected despite communist pressure.

Hungary

In 1945, free elections were held. The communists won some seats, but not enough to come to power. In 1947, after supposedly 'free' elections that they managed by intimidation, the communists were elected (for more on this see pages 22–25).

Poland

In free elections in 1945, a coalition of left-wing parties, including communists, came to power. Britain and the USA urged Stalin to take some Poles who had been in exile in London during the war into the government. He did so but, in 1947, after supposedly 'free' elections that they managed by intimidation, the communists took over entirely. The London Poles were executed or imprisoned or fled.

Romania

In 1945, as soon as the war ended, a coalition of left-wing parties, including many communists, took over in Romania. In February 1945, the king was forced to take a communist prime minister. By June, the communists were in control of the government. 'Free' elections in 1947 gave the communists complete control.

Czechoslovakia

In free elections in 1945, a coalition of left-wing parties, including communists, came to power. In 1946, the government was dominated by communists. But they could not win complete control in fair elections and began to lose, not gain, support. So, in 1948, they used the army to take over, having removed any officers who might object to doing so. Many non-communists were arrested, some were imprisoned, some executed.

Cominform: The Communist Information Bureau (1947)

In order to extend his control, Stalin established Cominform in 1947. Cominform was an international organisation that represented Communist Parties across Europe and brought them under the direction of the USSR.

The first Cominform Conference rejected the Marshall Plan. Consequently, Eastern European governments refused to accept Marshall Aid and Communist Parties in Western Europe were encouraged to organise strikes and demonstrations against the American plan. In France, for example, 2 million workers, sympathetic to the communists, went on strike in the winter of 1947, demanding that the French government reject Marshall Aid.

Cominform was also used to ensure the loyalty of Eastern European governments. It did this by investigating government ministers and employees, and removing those who were not loyal to Stalin.

This process was often violent. In Hungary, for example, 5% of the population was in prison by 1953. In this way, Cominform consolidated the power of the USSR through Eastern Europe by stamping out opposition and ensuring the loyalty of Eastern European governments.

Comecon: The Council for Mutual Economic Assistance (1949)

Comecon was Stalin's answer to the Marshall Plan. Stalin was aware that the Marshall Plan was very attractive to some Eastern European governments. Having ordered his satellite states to **boycott** Marshall Aid, he needed to set up a communist alternative. Therefore, in 1949 he established Comecon. In the first year, Comecon comprised the USSR, Bulgaria, Czechoslovakia, Hungary, Poland and Romania. Albania and Eastern Germany joined in 1950. Comecon aimed to encourage the economic development of Eastern Europe. It also attempted to prevent trade with Western Europe and America. This had political and economic implications.

- Politically, it would minimise American influence in Eastern Europe and the USSR.
- Economically, it ensured that the benefits of economic recovery in Eastern Europe remained within the Soviet 'sphere of influence'.
- It also meant that Eastern Europe did not have access to the prosperity of Western Europe.

'Two camps'

The USSR and America both recognised that, following the Potsdam Conference, Europe had divided into 'two camps'. This division had hardened as a result of Marshall Aid, which brought Western Europe into America's camp, and Cominform and Comecon, which established a Soviet camp in the East. In 1945, there had been two unofficial 'spheres of influence' in Europe. Marshall Aid and Comecon turned these 'spheres of influence' into two official economic alliances.

---

examzone

Watch out!

Do not confuse Cominform with Comecon. Remember Comecon is economic, and Cominform is political.

17

---

examzone

Build better answers

Exam question: Describe the key features of Cominform. (6 marks)

You need to make developed statements that answer the question and describe why the features mentioned in the answer are important.

■ **A basic answer (level 1):** One key feature of Cominform was that it allowed Stalin to control Eastern Europe.

● **A good answer (level 2):** One key feature of Cominform was that it allowed Stalin to control Eastern Europe. At Cominform's first conference, leaders of Eastern European countries agreed with Stalin to boycott Marshall Aid.

▲ **An excellent answer (full marks)** fully describes two or three key features.

Activity

Complete the following table, summarising the key features of Cominform and Comecon.

	Cominform	Comecon
Full name		
Date established		
Aims		
Effects		

The development of the Cold War: first confrontation

> ### Learning objectives
>
> In this chapter you will learn about:
> - the division of Germany into East and West
> - the impact of the Berlin Blockade
> - the formation of NATO and the arms race.

Germany: Unfinished business

Following the Second World War, Russia and America were unable to agree about the future of Germany. There were four key issues.

- Should a reunited Germany be part of the Soviet 'sphere of influence', the American 'sphere of influence', or should it be neutral?
- Should a reunited Germany have a communist or a capitalist government?
- Should a reunited Germany receive Marshall Aid?
- Should troops from America and the USSR be allowed to remain in a united Germany?

As they were unable to agree on the long-term future of Germany they agreed a short-term deal dividing Germany, and Germany's capital Berlin, into four zones. Each of the allies (the USA, the USSR, Britain and France) was responsible for the administration of one of the four zones.

Bizonia

By 1947, the British and American zones of Germany were essentially operating as one, and therefore became known as 'Bizonia' (meaning two zones). The relationship between Bizonia and the French zone was also very good, and therefore the three western zones were referred to as 'Trizonia'.

Although Germany's capital, Berlin, was deep within the Soviet zone, it too was divided into four regions, with the western section under American, French and British control.

	American zone
	British zone
	French zone
	Soviet zone

Division of Berlin

The division of Germany after the Second World War.

East and West Germany

The future of Germany was still the subject of intense negotiations between East and West. However, in 1948 the Western Allies started to develop a policy for western Germany that was at odds with Russia's plans. First, Britain, France and the USA agreed to set up a German assembly to create a German constitution. Secondly, they introduced a new currency – the Deutschmark – which would become the official currency for Trizonia.

Stalin had not been consulted about these developments and believed they were the first steps to creating a permanently divided Germany. He opposed the division of Germany for the following reasons.

- He was reluctant to allow America to have further influence over Germany.
- He did not want American troops to remain stationed in Germany.
- He realised that Germany's most valuable economic resources were in the west and feared that they would be used to wage war on the USSR.

The Berlin Blockade (1948–49)

In order to prevent the establishment of a separate state in western Germany, Stalin set up a military **blockade** around West Berlin in June 1948. His plan was to cut western Germany off from its capital (Berlin) so that the new government, based in Berlin, could not control its territory in western Germany. Stalin hoped that this would prove that a divided Germany could not work in practice.

President Truman responded with the 'Berlin Airlift'. Allied planes transported supplies to West Berlin around the clock. Initially, America committed 70 large cargo planes and airlifted between 600 and 700 tonnes of food and supplies every day. This had increased to 1000 tonnes a day within a couple of weeks. The British authorities maintained a similar system and, at its height, the airlift provided over 170,000 tonnes of supplies during January 1949.

The airlift prevented the blockade from succeeding. What is more, Truman's response was peaceful and made Stalin's military blockade appear highly aggressive.

The creation of the GDR and FRG

The Berlin Blockade was a propaganda success for the Americans, and an utter failure for the USSR. In May 1949, Stalin ended the blockade, and in September 1949, West Germany (officially called the Federal Republic of Germany, or FDR) was officially created as an independent state. One month later, the USSR established a second independent state – East Germany (officially known as the German Democratic Republic, or GDR). Soviet troops remained in the GDR, and the new country became another Soviet satellite state.

An aircraft participating in the Berlin airlift in 1949.

The Formation of NATO (1949)

The Berlin Blockade was the first military confrontation of the Cold War. It raised the possibility of a war in Europe. As a result, Western European nations tried to establish an alliance in order to 'keep the USA in, and the USSR out'. In April 1949, NATO (the North Atlantic Treaty Organisation) was established as an alliance between the USA and many of the countries in Western Europe. NATO members agreed that if any NATO country came under attack, all members of NATO would come to their defence.

The creation of NATO marked a significant development in the Cold War. The Marshall Plan had created a trading alliance but NATO went further. It was a military alliance with the specific aim of defending the West against communism.

The Formation of the Warsaw Pact (1955)

In 1955, the USSR responded to the creation of NATO by forming the Warsaw **Pact**, a military alliance of Eastern European countries that mirrored NATO. The eight Eastern European countries that made up the alliance included East Germany, Poland, Czechoslovakia and Hungary. The USSR already had Cominform but, when West Germany joined NATO, it was too provocative to ignore.

The arms race 1945–55

The arms race was an important feature of the Cold War. It included both a continuing commitment to maintaining a large army, navy and air force, and the development of ever-more-deadly nuclear weapons. In 1945, the USA became the first country to develop and use a nuclear bomb. By 1949, the USSR had caught up – it had developed and tested its own nuclear bomb. This prompted the Americans to develop hydrogen bombs – a second generation of more powerful nuclear weapons. By 1953, both countries had hydrogen bombs. However, the USA's warheads were still more powerful than those developed by the Soviet Union. Nonetheless, in 1955 the USSR tested a bomb known as 'Sakharov's Third Idea.' This new bomb was as powerful as America's hydrogen bombs.

These new bombs required either missiles or modified aircraft in order to attack enemy territory. By 1955, America had developed the **B52** Stratofortress, an aeroplane with the long-range flight capacity to bomb the Soviet Union. At the same time the Soviet Union was developing a similar aircraft known as the TU20 Bear.

Why was the arms race significant?

The arms race was significant because it prevented a war in Europe. The USSR had 3 million troops and could easily capture West Germany. However, the Soviet leaders would never order an invasion because they feared an American nuclear **retaliation**. One atomic bomb could turn an entire city into ashes and kill hundreds of thousands of people in a few seconds. Soviet leaders had paid close attention to the American bombings of Hiroshima and Nagasaki at the end of the Second World War and understood the awesome power of the new weapons.

NATO members: USA, Britain, Belgium, Canada, Denmark, France, Iceland, Italy, Luxembourg, Netherlands, Norway, Portugal, (Greece 1952, West Germany 1955)

Warsaw Pact: Soviet Union, Albania (until 1968), Bulgaria, Czechoslovakia, East Germany, Hungary, Poland, Romania

Did you know?

America and Russia named their nuclear bombs. Two of America's first nuclear bombs were named 'Fat Man' and 'Little Boy'. Russia named a bomb 'Layercake'.

Castle Romeo detonation, March 27 1954. Romeo was the third largest nuclear test carried out by the United States.

Source A

Source B

Activity

Sources A and B are from British newspapers published during the time of the Berlin Blockade and each shows a different message. The message in Source A is that the West is helping West Berlin with an airlift and increased supplies, whereas Stalin is sending nothing but 'lies', 'scares' and 'rumours' to threaten the West.

Source B likens the Berlin Blockade to a game of chess between Stalin and President Truman. Stalin's chess pieces are labelled '**Eastern Bloc**' and 'Berlin Blockade'. Truman's chess pieces are labeled 'Berlin Airlift' and 'Atlantic Pact'.

1 These cartoons offer a Western point of view. Now try to produce your own cartoon about the Berlin Airlift from a Soviet point of view.

examzone

Build better answers

Exam Question: How useful are Sources A and B as evidence of Russia's actions during the Berlin crisis? Explain your answer using Sources A and B and your own knowledge.

(10 marks)

■ **A basic answer (level 1)** makes simple comments on the content or provenance of the sources.

● **A good answer (level 2)** reaches a judgement about the usefulness of the sources based on their content or origin.

▲ **An excellent answer (level 3)** reaches a judgement about the usefulness of the sources based on their content or origin, and linking these to the purpose stated in the question. In addition, an excellent answer makes use of own knowledge to support its argument.

Hungary under Soviet rule: liberation and oppression

22

> ## Learning objectives
>
> In this chapter you will learn about:
> - the effect of Soviet rule on Hungary
> - the causes and consequences of 'de-Stalinisation'
> - the impact of the Hungarian revolt of 1956.

Hungary under Stalin

Stalin claimed that Soviet troops had liberated Hungary from the Nazis. However, in 1949, Cominform imposed an oppressive regime on Hungary.

- Hungarian land was redistributed to other Eastern European countries.
- Hungarian coal, oil and wheat were shipped to Russia while Hungarian citizens were deprived of food.
- Non-communist political parties were abolished.
- Russian officials controlled the government, the police and the army.
- Cominform began a reign of terror, executing popular political leaders and their supporters.
- Matyas Rakosi was appointed as Hungary's dictator.

Matyas Rakosi

Rakosi was Hungary's dictator from 1949 to 1956. He described himself as 'Stalin's best pupil' but the people of Hungary nicknamed him 'the bald butcher'. He developed what were known as 'salami tactics' for dealing with his opponents 'slice by slice', meaning he got rid of opposition by dividing it bit by bit. His oppressive regime imprisoned 387,000 and was responsible for more than 2,000 deaths.

'De-Stalinisation'

Stalin's death in 1953 was a turning point in the Cold War. Stalin's style of government, which is known as 'Stalinism', was extraordinarily oppressive. For example, it is believed that Stalin was responsible for the deaths of around 20 million people during his time in power. Russia's new leader, Nikita Khrushchev, opened the way for a more liberal approach to governing the USSR and Eastern Europe. In 1956, he gave the 'Secret Speech'. This speech, which did not remain secret for very long, promised an end to Stalinism throughout the entire Soviet sphere of influence.

Matyas Rakosi.

examzone
Top tip

In this section you have learned about three American presidents and two Russian leaders. The examiners will know which leaders are relevant to each question — you cannot get away with guessing. Make sure that you know who was in charge and when.

Activity

Use the information on pages 22–25 to create a timeline of the events in Hungary 1949–56.

Imre Nagy

Nagy had fought in the First World War and was captured and imprisoned by the Russians. He escaped from prison and fought for the Bolsheviks in the Russian Revolution. This was when he became a communist.

In 1919, Nagy joined the communist uprising in Hungary led by Bela Kun and funded by the USSR. Their takeover was quickly defeated and the new government was anti-communist. Nagy moved from place to place to avoid arrest, in Hungary and neighbouring countries. He returned to the USSR in 1929 and studied agriculture in Moscow.

Nagy returned to Hungary in 1944 and became involved in politics as a supporter of the USSR. In 1945, he was made Minister of Agriculture and set up land reforms to move the country towards collectivisation (state ownership of all the land). However, his concern for the welfare of the peasants (rather than the state) led to him being excluded from the Communist Party in 1949. After he made a public announcement of his support for the USSR, Nagy was allowed back into government.

He replaced Rakosi as Prime Minister between 1953 and 1955 (although Rakosi kept much of the real power, as Secretary of the Communist Party). In 1955, Nagy was again thrown out of the Communist Party for his opposition to Rakosi's tactics. Rakosi became Prime Minister, as well as Party Secretary, again

Nagy's programme of reform

Hungary's people were clearly dissatisfied with Soviet rule.

- Khrushchev's 'Secret Speech' created hopes of reform in Hungary. But nothing happened. Rakosi was forced out of power in July 1956, but still nothing happened.
- Bad harvests, and fuel and bread shortages, led to riots in Budapest on 23 October 1956. Students demonstrated in Parliament Square against the government and called for a 16-point list of reforms. Fighting broke out between students and police. This rapidly developed into a conflict that pulled in workers and even some members of the army, spreading from Budapest across the country.

To calm the situation, Khrushchev agreed to make Nagy Prime Minister and to withdraw the Red Army from Hungary. On 31 October 1956, Nagy announced his proposed reforms, which included Hungary's leaving the Warsaw Pact and holding free elections. Reformers made these bold moves because they hoped for support from the West.

- They asked the UN to recognise them as a neutral country. This would mean that any Soviet army entering Hungary would be breaking the rules of the UN, and so the UN could send in troops to remove them. The UN tried to intervene, but the USSR took no notice.
- The USA spent a lot of time encouraging Eastern European countries to get rid of their communist governments. US promises of aid were seen as promises of military help. The US-sponsored Radio Free Europe urged people to take a stand against their 'communist oppressors'. However, the aid the USA promised stopped short of military help because its highest priority was preventing a nuclear war with the USSR that would cause world-wide destruction.

The government split. Janos Kadar, a supporter of the USSR, set up a rival government in eastern Hungary.

Khrushchev responds to Nagy

Nagy's reforms ended Hungary's alliance with the USSR. Khrushchev believed that the reforms were unacceptable and that if Hungary was allowed to leave the Warsaw Pact, other Eastern European countries would soon follow. Indeed, Khrushchev had access to secret intelligence reports which indicated that discontent with communism was widespread across Eastern Europe. These reports reinforced his view that allowing greater freedom for these discontented countries could mean the end of Soviet dominance in Eastern Europe.

Khrushchev responded with a decisive show of force. On 4 November 1956, 200,000 Soviet troops and 1,000 tanks entered Hungary in support of Kadar's government. They marched on Budapest, where they fought with supporters of Nagy's government, through two weeks of bitter fighting.

- About 2,500 people were killed by the Soviet troops and about 20,000 were wounded.
- Almost 200,000 fled to the West.

- About 650 Soviet troops were killed and about 1,250 were wounded.

The trouble rumbled on into 1957, with strikes in various parts of the country and outbreaks of fighting. But the revolution was really over in November.

Nagy's trial and execution

Nagy sought protection in the Yugoslavian embassy. The Yugoslavian ambassador agreed with Khrushchev that Nagy was free to leave Hungary. However, as soon as Nagy left the embassy, he was arrested by Soviet troops. Nagy was accused of treason and, in a trial overseen by Khrushchev, was found guilty. He was hanged in June 1958. Following his execution, Khrushchev stated that Nagy's fate was 'a lesson to the leaders of all socialist countries'.

The international reaction

Following Nagy's arrest, America offered food and medical aid worth $20 million to Hungary and allowed 80,000 Hungarian **refugees** to move to the USA. President Dwight D. Eisenhower (1953–61) praised the bravery of the Hungarian people and encouraged them to fight on.

The UN officially condemned the Soviet invasion and conducted a thorough enquiry into it, but did nothing more. Spain, the Netherlands and Sweden boycotted the 1956 Olympics in protest at Soviet action in Hungary and thousands of people left the communist parties of many European countries. The USA's failure to support the Hungarians showed its commitment to liberating Europe from communism did not include military support. Consequently, radicals in Eastern Europe were discouraged from following Hungary's example.

examzone
Top tip

Detailed answers tend to gain higher marks than answers that are vague. One good way of making answers more detailed is to include names. For example, rather than saying 'the American president' in a question relating to the Soviet invasion of Hungary, you could say 'President Eisenhower'.

Activity

It is November 1956. Kadar has been in power for one month. The people below are reflecting on how the events in Hungary have affected them and changed the balance of power in the Cold War. Complete their thought bubbles to show what they are thinking.

Eisenhower   Khrushchev   Kadar   a Hungarian revolutionary

Reasserting Soviet control

Following the Soviet invasion, Khrushchev appointed Janos Kadar as the new Hungarian leader. Initially, Kadar had no real power as Hungary was under the control of the Soviet army. Nonetheless, Kadar published his Fifteen-Point Programme setting out the new government's direction. Kadar's programme included:

- re-establishing communist control of Hungary
- using Hungarian troops to stop attacks on Soviet forces
- remaining in the Warsaw Pact
- negotiating the withdrawal of Soviet troops once the crisis was over.

The Hungarian people soon accepted Kadar's new government. America's failure to support Nagy's government left them with no choice.

Activities

1 Use the information in Key Topic 1 of this book to produce a timeline of the changing relationship between Russia and America in the period 1943–56.

2 Using the information on your timeline, select the three events that you feel led to the greatest change in the relationship between Russia and America.

3 In each case, highlight the event and write a short paragraph explaining how this event changed the relationship and why it was so important.

examzone
Build better answers

Exam question: Explain why relations between the Soviet Union and the USA changed in the years 1943–56. (13 marks)
You may use the following in your answer.
- Roosevelt's death
- The effects of the Truman Doctrine
You must also include information of your own.

You need to make relevant points, supported by specific examples, with a clear focus on how each factor led to the situation described.
In each level, the number of statements you make will affect the quality of your answer. For example, in level 2, a single developed argument is unlikely to provide as complete an answer as three developed arguments.

■ **A basic answer (level 1)** is correct, but does not have details to support it (for example, *One reason why the relationship between the Soviet Union and the USA changed was because of Roosevelt's death*).

● **A good answer (level 2)** provides the details as well but does not explain how they caused the event process mentioned in the question (for example, *One reason why the relationship between the Soviet Union and the USA changed was because of Roosevelt's death. Roosevelt had been prepared to work with Stalin at the Teheran and Yalta Conferences*).

▲ **A better answer (level 3)** provides reasons, supports these with detail and explains how they caused the event process mentioned in the question (for example, *One reason why the relationship between the Soviet Union and the USA changed was because of Roosevelt's death. Roosevelt had been prepared to work with Stalin at the Teheran and Yalta Conferences. Following his death, the new president – Truman – was very suspicious of Stalin and was less willing to work with him. This led to a change in the relationship because, whilst Roosevelt had been willing to work with Stalin, his successor Truman was much more reluctant to compromise*).

▲ **An excellent answer (level 4)** shows how the reasons are linked and/or reaches a judgement about their relative importance.

Make sure you write accurately – there are 3 extra marks available for spelling, grammar and punctuation in these questions.
Now write another paragraph in answer to this question. Choose one of the points mentioned below, add examples, explain how this factor changed relations between the Soviet Union and the USA in the period stated, and explain how this factor is linked to the factor discussed above and reach a judgement about which of the two factors is most important.
- the effects of the Truman Doctrine
- disagreement over the future of Germany
- the creation of NATO and the Warsaw Pact.

Key Topic 2: Three Cold War crises: Berlin, Cuba and Czechoslovakia *c.1957-69*

Between 1958 and 1962, the world faced what President John F. Kennedy called a period of 'maximum danger'. Indeed, the world faced annihilation in a nuclear war twice in these years. After 1963, tensions began to ease but the Cold War was still far from over.

In this section you will study three Cold War flashpoints:

- the Berlin Crisis of 1958–63
- the Cuban Missile Crisis of 1962
- Czechoslovakia and the Prague Spring, 1968–69.

You will see how the disputed status of Berlin and the development of the arms race took the world to the brink of **nuclear holocaust**. Additionally, you will consider how tensions in Eastern Europe led to the most significant challenge to Soviet authority since the Hungarian crisis of 1956.

The Berlin Crisis: a divided city

Learning objectives

In this chapter you will learn about:

- the refugee problem facing the East German government
- Khrushchev's ultimatum of 1958.

Following the Second World War, the USSR and America had been unable to agree on how Germany should be governed. Consequently, Germany had been divided but the USSR refused to recognise West Germany and America refused to acknowledge East Germany. The city of Berlin caused problems as it was partly controlled by the Americans although it was located inside the Eastern Bloc – those countries belonging to the Warsaw Pact. See the map on page 29, showing the division of Berlin.

Refugee problems

The East German government was extremely unpopular and therefore many East Germans fled to West Germany. West Germany was highly attractive as its citizens enjoyed greater freedom and wealth than those of East Germany. Indeed, between 1949 and 1961, 2.7 million East German refugees, many of whom were highly skilled, escaped to West Germany. Berlin was the centre of East Germany's refugee problem because it was easy for East Germans to get from East Berlin to West Berlin, and from there to West Germany.

Khrushchev's ultimatum

The refugee problem was a propaganda disaster for Khrushchev because it proved that many people preferred the capitalist West to the communist East. For this reason, in November 1958, Khrushchev declared that the whole of the city of Berlin officially belonged to East Germany. He also issued an ultimatum, giving US troops six months to withdraw. Khrushchev's plan was to prevent East Germans fleeing to the West and to humiliate the USA.

Exam question: Outline two reasons why Khrushchev demanded the withdrawal of American troops from Berlin in 1958.   (4 marks)
You need to make two developed statements. These are statements that answer the question and provide some additional detail.

◼ **A basic answer (level 1):**
Khrushchev wanted to stop so many East Germans leaving. Also Khrushchev wanted control over the whole of the city.

● **A good answer (4 marks)**
Khrushchev wanted to stop so many East Germans leaving via West Berlin. Almost 3 million Germans had chosen to leave communist Eastern Europe for the capitalist West. Also Khrushchev wanted control over the whole of the city as part of a plan to demonstrate the power of the Soviet Union and humiliate America.

Activity

It is November 1958. You are one of President Eisenhower's top advisors. You are helping Eisenhower to decide how to respond to Khrushchev's ultimatum. From the list on the right, choose two options: the one you believe to be most appropriate, and the one you feel would be least effective. Write a paragraph for each, explaining why you believe Eisenhower should or shouldn't take this course of action.

Possible courses of action:

- Hold a **summit** meeting to try to persuade Khrushchev to change his mind.
- Withdraw American troops from Berlin.
- Invade Eastern Germany.
- Agree to withdraw troops only if Khrushchev withdraws his troops from East Germany.
- Do nothing.

The Berlin Crisis: negotiation and stalemate

> ### Learning objectives
>
> In this chapter you will learn about:
>
> • the failure of negotiations with Khrushchev over the future of Berlin
> • Khrushchev's ultimatum and Kennedy's preparation for war.

Eisenhower's response

In November 1958, Khrushchev demanded that the Western powers remove their troops from West Berlin within six months. The Americans were uncertain about how to respond to this. Eisenhower did not want to lose West Berlin, but neither did he want to start a war. Consequently it was agreed to hold an international meeting in order to discuss Berlin's future.

The Geneva Summit

That meeting took place in May 1959. Talks were held in a 'summit' meeting in Geneva between foreign representatives from the USA and the USSR. No solution to the problem was agreed at this meeting. However it did lay the groundwork for Khrushchev to visit the USA and hold face-to-face talks with Eisenhower.

Eisenhower and Camp David

In September 1959 Khrushchev and Eisenhower met at a second summit meeting in Camp David, the US presidential country retreat. During the Camp David Summit, the two leaders spoke frankly. Despite not agreeing a solution to the problems, it was decided that a further summit meeting would be held the following year between the two leaders. Additionally Khrushchev agreed to withdraw his six-month ultimatum.

The Paris Summit

This meeting took place in Paris in May 1960, but was a disaster. Just before the conference the USSR had shot down an American spy plane over Russia and captured its pilot. Khrushchev walked out of the conference in protest when Eisenhower refused to apologise for the incident.

The Vienna Conference

When John F. Kennedy became the new president of the USA in January 1961, a further summit was arranged to discuss Berlin. At the Vienna Conference of June 1961, neither side seemed willing to back down over the US presence in Berlin. However, Khrushchev saw Kennedy's inexperience as a weakness to be exploited. Confident that Kennedy would back down if pushed, Khrushchev once again gave the USA a six-month ultimatum to remove its troops from Berlin.

Khrushchev and Kennedy at the Vienna Conference in June 1961.

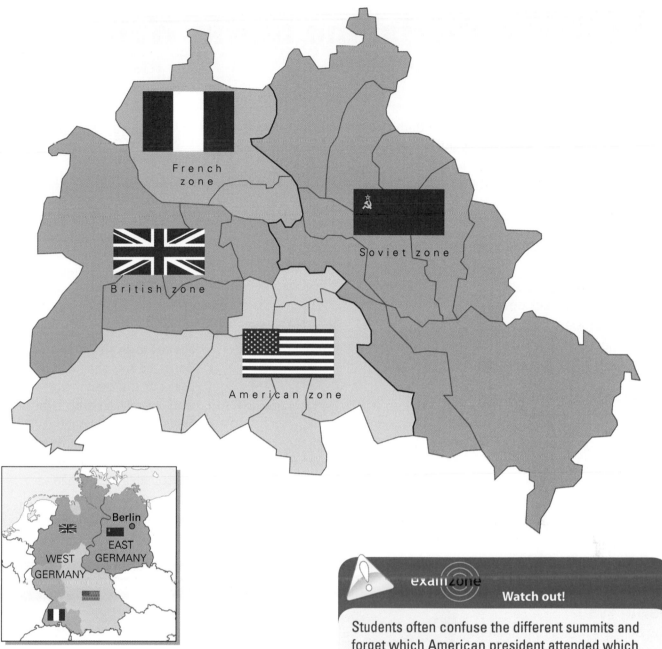

Map showing the division of Berlin into American, British, French and Soviet zones and, inset, the location of Berlin within Soviet-controlled East Germany.

exam zone

Watch out!

Students often confuse the different summits and forget which American president attended which summit. You could draw a timeline to help you to remember this information.

Kennedy prepares for war

Despite Khrushchev's ultimatum, Kennedy refused to back down. He declared that he would not remove American troops from Berlin. He also started preparing America for war, committing the US government to an additional $3.2 billion of defence spending. More worrying still was Kennedy's decision to spend an extra $207 million on building nuclear **fallout shelters**. A point of stalemate had been reached.

Activity

Design a propaganda poster on behalf of the American government, justifying the increased spending on defence and fallout shelters. Ensure that you explain why this money needs to be spent, how it will benefit the American population, and how it will help to promote world peace.

The Berlin Crisis: the Berlin Wall

> **Learning objectives**
>
> In this chapter you will learn about:
> - the reasons for the creation of the Berlin Wall
> - Kennedy's response to the building of the Berlin Wall.

Building the wall

Khrushchev knew that the USSR could not win a nuclear war. In 1961, America had almost 20 times more nuclear weapons than the USSR. What is more, American nuclear weapons were able to reach the USSR, whereas Soviet weapons could not reach America. Kennedy's refusal to retreat called Khrushchev's bluff, forcing the Russian leader to back down.

Khrushchev could not force the Americans to leave West Berlin but he still had to solve the refugee problem. His solution was to build a wall separating East and West Berlin, making it impossible for East Germans to escape to the West.

On the night of 12 August 1961, East German troops secretly erected a barbed wire fence around the whole of West Berlin. The next morning, Berliners awoke to a divided city. In the coming months the fence was reinforced and eventually became a heavily guarded wall. Soviet tanks were deployed to block further Western access to the East, causing a day-long stand-off with US tanks on 27 October. Finally, after 18 hours, the tanks began to pull back – one by one. The crisis had passed. Kennedy commented 'it's not a very nice solution, but a wall is a hell of a lot better than a war'.

Did you know?

There were numerous attempts to cross the Berlin Wall, many of which ended in tragedy. Peter Fechter, for example, planned to cross the wall to West Germany in 1962. He jumped from a window into the 'death strip' between the East and West sides of the wall. However, during his attempt to climb into West Berlin, he was shot. He fell back into the 'death strip', where he lay screaming for help for almost an hour while he bled to death. Guards on the Western side of the wall were unable to help him as they knew this would trigger further violence from guards on the East.

The impact of the Berlin Wall

The Berlin Wall was significant for the following reasons:

- it stopped East Germans escaping to the West and therefore ended the refugee crisis
- it allowed Khrushchev to avoid war with America while still appearing strong
- it became a powerful symbol of the division of Germany and the division of Europe.

The building of the Berlin Wall.

Kennedy making a speech during his visit to Berlin, 1963.

Kennedy's visit to Berlin

Kennedy was unable to prevent the wall's construction. However, in 1963 he toured West Berlin expressing his feelings of solidarity with its people. Crowds of West Germans lined the streets shouting 'Kenne-dy – Kenne-dy!' In a famous speech, Kennedy said 'All free men, wherever they live, are citizens of Berlin and therefore as a free man, I take pride in the words *Ich bin ein Berliner*'. West Berlin had become a symbol of freedom.

Activities

1 Copy and cut out the cards on the right.

2 Group the cards into those that describe causes of the building of the Berlin Wall, and those that describe consequences of the building of the Berlin Wall.

3 For each group, decide which cause/consequence was the most important and write a sentence explaining why.

The USSR realised it could not win a nuclear war.	The East German economy lost skilled labourers.	The problem of the division of Berlin was solved.
Refugees were unable to leave East Germany.	Many people from East Germany escaped to West Germany.	Khrushchev avoided war with America.
The East German government was unpopular.	Kennedy refused to back down.	Peter Fechter was killed.
An important symbol of the Cold War was created.	Kennedy showed solidarity with the people of West Berlin.	Kennedy increased the USA's defence budget.

The Cuban Missile Crisis: origins

> ## Learning objectives
>
> In this chapter you will learn about:
> - the development of the arms race between 1945 and 1961
> - the effects of Cuba's revolution
> - Khrushchev's decision to build missile bases on Cuba.

> ## Did you know?
>
> Communism is associated with the colour red. One symbol of communism is the red star and the flag of the Soviet Union was red. Throughout the Cold War period Americans often referred to communists as 'reds'.

The developing arms race

America was the clear winner of the **arms race** in the 1940s and 1950s. America had an early lead and dropped the first nuclear bombs on the Japanese cities of Hiroshima and Nagasaki in August 1945. By 1949, the USSR was producing atomic bombs too. The arms race to develop and stockpile nuclear weapons was a big part of the Cold War. If the Cold War became actual war, then both governments expected that nuclear weapons would be used. In the USA, schools held regular 'duck and cover' rehearsals of what to do in case of nuclear attack. By 1960, Britain and France had nuclear weapons too and China was running a nuclear weapon development programme. In theory, it would soon be far too destructive for either side to use their nuclear weapons. But neither side trusted the other enough to stop the race; and each mistrusted the other side enough to fear they just might attack.

Both sides produced 'statistics' about their nuclear capacity, much of which was designed to frighten the other side, rather than reflect the real situation. Also, statistics could be confused – the number of weapons was not the only consideration; there was also the size of their warheads and the accuracy with which they were aimed.

American B52 bombers.

The Tsar Bomba.

Did you know?

The largest nuclear bomb ever tested was detonated in 1961. The Russian *Tsar Bomba* was eight metres long and weighed 27 tons. The bomb was more than 100 times more powerful than the American weapons detonated in Japan at the end of the Second World War. When it was tested, it created a fireball 8 kilometres (5 miles) in diameter.

The table below gives statistics that are widely used for arms holdings in 1960. However, some historians think that the USSR's figures are overestimated. Nonetheless, the table shows what many people in the USA and the USSR believed the situation was at the time.

Source A: Nuclear capacity of the superpowers in 1960

Nuclear capacity	USA	USSR
Inter-continental ballistic missile (long-range airborne)	450	76
Mid-range airborne ballistic missile	250	700
Nuclear submarine	32	12
Long-range bombers able to carry nuclear weapons	2,260	1,600

Each country had particular areas of concern.

- The USA's biggest concern was the rate at which the USSR was building nuclear weapons – and the size of those weapons. The *Tsar Bomba*, detonated in 1961, was the most powerful, and therefore most destructive, bomb ever.
- The USSR's biggest concern was that US missiles were much closer to the USSR than its missiles were to the US. In 1958, the USA arranged to have nuclear missiles at their UK bases. In 1961, their bases in Italy and Turkey received nuclear weapons too. These could easily be fixed on specific targets, such as Moscow. The USSR could fire missiles at the USA, but the missiles had to travel further, which meant they could not be targeted anywhere near as accurately.

What is more, America had specially equipped **B52 bombers** that were capable of dropping nuclear weapons on the Soviet Union.

The USSR had relatively few missiles and no way of dropping them accurately on American soil. Nonetheless, the US government was extremely worried about the Soviet Union's nuclear capabilities.

Exam-style question

Give two reasons from Source A which show that America was ahead in the nuclear arms race in 1960.

(2 marks)

Activities

1 Copy the table below.
2 Use the information in 'The developing arms race' section of this chapter to complete the second column of the table, explaining why America was in a stronger position than it thought.

America is worried that…	But the real situation is that…
… Sputnik 1 proves that the USSR has very powerful missiles.	
… the USSR can land a spaceship on the moon, therefore it could put nuclear missiles in space.	
… Khrushchev has said that the USSR is producing missiles as fast as it is producing sausages.	

In 1957, Russian scientists launched Sputnik 1 – the world's first man-made satellite. By 1960, the Russians had even landed a robotic spacecraft on the moon. Khrushchev boasted that the Americans were 'sleeping under a red moon'. This demonstrated the sophistication of Soviet technology, and many Americans believed that the rockets used to put satellites in space could be used to launch nuclear missiles at America.

However, the USSR was simply not wealthy enough to mass-produce missiles and Khrushchev's claim that the USSR was 'producing missiles like we are producing sausages' was an empty boast.

The Cuban Revolution

Cuba had traditionally been an ally of the USA. American presidents believed that Cuba's friendship was important because it was only 145 kilometres (90 miles) away and therefore part of the American sphere of influence.

Much of the land in Cuba was owned by American businesses. According to a report by the US Department of Trade in 1956, US companies:

- ran 90% of the phone and electric supply
- ran 50% of the railways
- ran 40% of all sugar production
- owned and supplied all the oil refineries.

The Cuban Revolution of 1959 overthrew Cuba's pro-American government. The new revolutionary regime, led by Fidel Castro, wanted greater independence from the United States. As part of this policy, Castro's new government took over American property located in Cuba. In response, America banned the import of Cuban sugar. This threatened to bankrupt the Cuban economy.

January 1959	Castro went to the USA. President Eisenhower refused to see him or accept his government as the rightful government of Cuba.
May 1959	Castro's Land Reform Act banned foreign ownership of land. Other countries that owned land in Cuba accepted payment for this. The USA did not, because they did not accept that Castro's government had the right to pass laws.
January 1960	Castro took the land the USA would not take payment for.

February 1960	Castro made an agreement to sell the USSR sugar and buy its oil.
March 1960	Oil from the USSR arrived. The US-owned refineries refused to take it. Castro nationalised the oil refineries.
July 1960	The USA banned all trade with Cuba. Castro nationalised all US businesses in Cuba. The USSR agreed to buy more sugar, and provide more goods and loans.

Cuba turned to the USSR for help. Khrushchev was delighted to have an ally deep in America's sphere of influence. Consequently, he agreed to offer economic aid to Cuba in order to help his new ally industrialise.

The Bay of Pigs incident

John F. Kennedy became president of the USA in January 1961. By this point, the **CIA** had tried, and failed, to assassinate Castro several times and were increasingly concerned over Cuba's ties with the USSR. Americans did not want a communist country on their doorstep; certainly not one that had the USSR as an ally. The CIA persuaded Kennedy to launch an invasion of Cuba to dislodge Castro's government and put Batista (the old, corrupt ruler of Cuba who had been a US ally) back in charge. This invasion had been planned for over a year. They assured Kennedy that:

- they could make it look like a Cuban revolt, not a US invasion, as they had been training Cuban exiles in guerrilla fighting and they could disguise old US planes to look like Cuban ones for bombing
- Castro's hold on the country was weak
- most Cubans would join in against Castro once the invasion began.

Kennedy agreed to the plan. But the invasion was a disaster.

- The plan, supposedly secret, was known to Castro's government.
- Most Cubans did not want Batista back.
- The first strike by the disguised planes, on 15 April, missed most of its targets, including Castro's air base. The planes were photographed and US involvement was made public. Kennedy cancelled a planned second airstrike.

34

- The Cuban-exile army of about 1,400 invaded at the Bay of Pigs on 17 April. It was soon facing heavy air attacks and about 20,000 of Castro's troops. Kennedy sent in planes, but too late. The Cuban exiles, with not enough US help and no support from other Cubans, surrendered.

The Bay of Pigs ended any chance that the USA and Cuba might negotiate a friendly relationship. Castro declared himself a communist. The Americans began making fresh plans to overthrow Castro, and the USSR began to negotiate with Castro to provide military 'protection' that would, for the first time, place Soviet nuclear missiles very close to the USA.

Map showing Cuba in relation to the USA.

Missile bases

In spite of his victory, Castro felt vulnerable and feared another American attack. He therefore asked Khrushchev to help him defend Cuba. In August 1961, Khrushchev devised a plan that would solve the problems of both Cuba and Russia. He decided to station Russian nuclear weapons on Cuban soil. He claimed this would deter America from attempting another invasion. It would also place Russian nuclear missiles within striking range of America, balancing the US presence in Turkey. This meant that Khrushchev could attack America without spending large amounts of money developing inter-continental ballistic missiles.

Activity

Use the information in this chapter to draw a timeline of the key events of 1957–61, showing the build up to the Cuban Missile Crisis.

examzone

Build better answers

Exam question: Describe the key features of the arms race.

(6 marks)

You need to make two or three developed statements that answer the question, not simply write all you know. For example, a key feature of the arms race at this time is that it was a race about nuclear weapons.

■ **A basic answer (level 1):**
One key feature of the arms race was that both sides developed nuclear weapons. Another feature was that the USA was winning the arms race until the mid-1960s.

● **A good answer (level 2):**
One key feature of the arms race was that both sides developed nuclear weapons. For example, America was the first superpower to develop the atomic bomb and by the early 1960s they had modified B52 bombers so they were capable of dropping these bombs on the USSR. Another key feature was that the USA was winning the arms race until the mid-1960s. For example, the USA had 20 times more nuclear warheads than the Soviet Union.

The Cuban Missile Crisis: the 'Thirteen Days'

Learning objectives

In this chapter you will learn about:

- how America learned of Khrushchev's plan
- the 'hawks' and the 'doves'
- the events of the 'Thirteen Days'.

Did you know?

Robert McNamara, the Secretary of Defence at the time of the Cuban Missile Crisis, was asked how close the USA and the USSR came to war over Cuba. He replied: 'I thought I might never live to see another Saturday night.'

The Thirteen Days

The 'Thirteen Days' was the period in 1962 at the height of the Cuban Missile Crisis during which there seemed to be the greatest threat of nuclear war.

The events of the 'Thirteen Days' of 1962:

16 Oct	Kennedy is informed of Khrushchev's plans to place nuclear missiles on Cuba.
20 Oct	Kennedy decides to impose a naval blockade around Cuba to prevent further missiles reaching Cuba.
22 Oct	Kennedy gives a public address officially declaring the blockade and calling on Khrushchev to recall his ships.
23 Oct	Khrushchev sends a letter to Kennedy stating that Soviet ships will break through the blockade.
24 Oct	Soviet ships approach the line of blockade (500 miles from Cuba). At 10.32am the closest ships suddenly stop or turn around. Khrushchev issues a statement that the USSR is prepared to launch nuclear weapons if America goes to war.
25 Oct	American and Soviet armed forces are on the highest level of alert – they are told to prepare for war. Kennedy writes to Khrushchev asking him to withdraw missiles from Cuba.
26 Oct	Khrushchev responds to Kennedy's letter, saying that he will withdraw Soviet missiles in return for a guarantee that the USA will not invade Cuba.
27 Oct	Khrushchev receives intelligence that the USA is planning to invade Cuba in 24 hours. He proposes a deal: the USSR will withdraw missiles from Cuba if the USA will agree never to invade Cuba and withdraw its nuclear missiles from Turkey.
	An American spy plane is shot down over Cuba. American 'hawks' demand **retaliation**.
	Robert Kennedy (Kennedy's brother and chief advisor) approaches the Russian ambassador accepting Khrushchev's deal but demands that the withdrawal of American missiles from Turkey is kept secret.
28 Oct	Khrushchev accepts this secret deal.

Khrushchev's plan is revealed

On 25 September 1962, Khrushchev sent 114 Soviet ships to Cuba. The ships carried a secret cargo, including nuclear warheads and long-range missiles, that would be used to construct nuclear bases on Cuba. For a long time, Khrushchev's plan remained secret. But by mid-October American spy planes had discovered what was going on. On 22 October Kennedy addressed the American people and told them of the Soviet plans to build nuclear missile bases on their doorstep.

Kennedy's news shocked the world. Many Americans panicked and started building nuclear shelters in preparation for nuclear war. A fleet of nuclear submarines was prepared by the US Navy and 156 ICBMs were primed for launch.

'Hawks' and 'doves'

During the crisis, Kennedy and Khrushchev's advisors were split into two groups: hawks and doves. The 'hawks' on both sides wanted an aggressive policy. Some American generals, for example, believed that a nuclear war between the USA and the USSR was inevitable and therefore Kennedy should go to war because, as things stood, America had a good chance of winning. The 'doves', on the other hand, advised caution, recommending diplomatic strategies, which they felt offered the best chance of peace.

Images taken by US spy planes of nuclear missile bases being built in Cuba. The images were released in 1962.

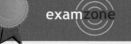

Activities

1 Copy and complete the table below, explaining how the statements apply to the USA, the USSR or both.

	USA	USSR	Both
Cuban Missile Crisis was a success			
Cuban Missile Crisis was a failure			

2 Write a paragraph that explains who gained most from the Cuban Missile Crisis. Make sure that you back up your point with detailed examples.

The Cuban Missile Crisis: immediate and long-term consequences

Learning objectives

In this chapter you will learn about:

● the immediate consequences of the Cuban Missile Crisis, including the creation of the 'hotline', the Test Ban Treaty and détente

● the long-term consequences of the Cuban Missile Crisis, including the doctrine of Mutually Assured Destruction (MAD) and the French decision to leave NATO.

The immediate consequences of the Cuban Missile Crisis

The first consequence of the Cuban Missile Crisis was the reduction in Khrushchev's authority. Because the removal of American missiles from Turkey remained secret, it seemed to many that he had backed down and betrayed his allies in Cuba.

The Cuban Missile Crisis had highlighted the fragility of international peace and the difficulties of negotiation between Russia and America in a crisis situation. As a result, the superpowers agreed to the introduction of the following measures:

● the 'hotline' – in June 1963, a direct communications link was set up between the American President in Washington and the Russian Premier in Moscow

● the Limited Test Ban Treaty – in August 1963, the USA and USSR agreed to ban the testing of all nuclear weapons in space, in the sea and above ground. Underground nuclear tests were still permitted.

The Test Ban Treaty was the first step taken to control the use of nuclear weapons. Once there was agreement on this, the way was open to discuss limiting weapon production and cutting down stockpiles.

President Kennedy signalled his commitment to working with the USSR in a speech of June 1963, in which he argued that both superpowers needed to focus on their 'common interests'. This speech was the beginning of a policy called 'détente': a relaxing of tension in the relationship between the USA and the USSR. Initially, moves to détente were slow but détente became a key feature of superpower relations during the 1970s.

HERBLOCK'S CARTOON

"Let's Get A Lock For This Thing"

NUCLEAR WAR

Source A: A cartoon from the Washington Post, *published on 1 November 1962.*

The long-term consequences of the Cuban Missile Crisis

The leaders of the Soviet Union were determined never again to be pushed around by America. Therefore, the Soviet government made every effort to catch up with America in the arms race. By 1965, the USA and the USSR were on an equal footing in terms of their nuclear capability. This created greater stability in the relationship between the two superpowers. American and Russian leaders realised that any nuclear war was bound to destroy both countries. This idea, known as the doctrine of Mutually Assured Destruction (MAD), gave both superpowers an excellent reason for avoiding war.

Another long-term consequence of the Cuban Missile Crisis was the French decision to leave NATO. In the event of a nuclear war between America and Russia, the members of NATO would be obliged to fight alongside America. French President Charles de Gaulle was appalled at the thought that France would be destroyed in this way. Therefore, in 1966, France ended its military alliance with America and began to develop its own nuclear missiles.

Did you know?

The 'hotline' between the American President and the Soviet Premier is sometimes known as the 'red telephone'. Despite this, it was originally a teleprinter system. It was first used in 1967, and in 1971 it was upgraded and became an actual telephone. It is still used today, and is tested every hour of every day.

Activities

Source B: From a speech by President Kennedy on 10 June 1963.
Let us direct attention to our common interests [with the Soviet Union] and to the means by which our differences can be resolved. Our most basic common link is that we all inhabit this small planet. We all breathe the same air. We all cherish our children's future.

Exam-style question

How useful are Sources A and B as evidence of the consequences of the Cuban Missile Crisis of October 1962. **(10 marks)**

Activities

1 Divide the class into two groups. One group should study the immediate consequences of the Cuban Missile Crisis. The other group should study the long-term consequences of the Cuban Missile Crisis.

2 Divide each group into pairs. Each pair should produce a ten-minute lesson designed to teach a pair from the other group about the topic they have been studying.

Each lesson should include:

- an interesting activity to enable the 'students' to learn about the topic
- an activity designed to assess what the 'students' have learned
- feedback, based on the assessment, explaining what the 'students' know well and targets for improvement.

3 Join with a pair from the other group, and take it in turns to teach your lesson.

Czechoslovakia: 'Prague Spring'

> **Learning objectives**
>
> In this chapter you will learn about:
> - Czechoslovakian opposition to Soviet control
> - Dubcek's attitude to communism
> - the reforms of the 'Prague Spring'.

Czechoslovakian opposition to Soviet control

There are strong similarities between what happened in Hungary in 1956 and events in Czechoslovakia 12 years later.

Czechoslovakia was a Soviet satellite state. Communism had had few benefits for the Czech people. In the mid-1960s, Czechoslovakia was still run by the secret police, which brutally crushed all political opposition. At the same time, the Czechoslovakian economy was struggling. Therefore the majority of Czech people suffered a declining standard of living during the 1960s.

Political repression and economic problems made Communist Party leader Antonin Novotny highly unpopular, and as a result his leadership was challenged. On 5 January 1968, Alexander Dubcek became the Communist Party leader: the most powerful man in Czechoslovakia.

Dubcek

Dubcek was the natural choice to lead Czechoslovakia. He was a committed communist who was on friendly terms with Leonid Brezhnev (the Russian leader following Khrushchev's fall from power in 1964). Dubcek's aim was to create a genuinely popular form of communism. He described this as 'socialism with a human face'. Essentially, Dubcek wanted to get rid of the most repressive aspects of communist rule, to reform the economy and to allow more cultural freedom. In this way, he hoped to revitalise Czechoslovakian politics, economics and social life.

Czechoslovakia and the USSR.

Communist Governments affiliated to the USSR

The reforms of the 'Prague Spring'

'Prague Spring' is a phrase used to describe the liberal changes brought about by Dubcek from April 1968. It was named after the city of Prague, the Czechoslovakian capital. As part of his plan to create 'socialism with a human face', Dubcek introduced the following reforms:

- a relaxation of press censorship
- the legalisation of political opposition groups
- official government toleration of political criticism
- more power given to regional governments
- more power given to the Czech parliament
- 'market socialism' – the reintroduction of capitalist elements into the Czech economy.

Dubcek said that his aim was to allow 'the widest possible democracy in the social and political life of Czechoslovakia'. Dubcek's reforms were welcomed enthusiastically by students, intellectuals, workers and younger members of the Czech Communist Party. Artists and writers such as Milan Kundera and Vaclav Havel took full advantage of the reforms, writing books, plays, and essays critical of Soviet-style communism.

Older Czechoslovakian communists were shocked by the 'Prague Spring' and their horror was shared by Soviet Premier Brezhnev and his allies across Eastern Europe.

examzone
Build better answers

Exam question: Describe one reason why Dubcek introduced reforms in Czechoslovakia.

(2 marks)

■ **A basic answer (level 1)** is accurate but lacks detail.

● **A good answer (level 2)** is accurate and includes supporting information.

The following is a basic level 1 answer to the exam question above. Add supporting information to turn it into a good answer.

Dubcek introduced reforms because he wanted to solve Czechoslovakia's economic problems.

Activity

Imagine that you are one of Dubcek's speechwriters. Write a speech for him to deliver to the Czechoslovakian Communist Party, introducing his reforms and explaining why the 'Prague Spring' will help the Party to become more popular.

You may wish to refer to the problems experienced in other communist countries, for example East Germany and Hungary.

Czechoslovakia: the Brezhnev Doctrine

> ### Learning objectives
>
> In this chapter you will learn about:
> - the re-establishment of Soviet control in Czechoslovakia
> - the Brezhnev Doctrine
> - the Soviet invasion of Czechoslovakia.

Brezhnev's dilemma

The 'Prague Spring' made life very difficult for Soviet Premier Brezhnev. On the one hand, he regarded Dubcek as a friend, and Dubcek had made no attempt to leave the Warsaw Pact or damage the USSR. On the other hand, secret Soviet intelligence reports suggested that Dubcek's reforms would lead to a weakening of Soviet control over Czechoslovakia and, in the long run, the break-up of the Eastern Bloc.

From April through to July, Brezhnev was in constant contact with Dubcek and attempted to persuade him that the reforms had gone too far. However, Dubcek failed to take the hint and took little action to control political opposition in Czechoslovakia. By late August, Brezhnev had had enough and ordered a full-scale invasion of Czechoslovakia in order to overthrow Dubcek.

The Brezhnev Doctrine

Throughout August 1968, the Soviet media portrayed Czechoslovakia as a massive threat to the USSR. Brezhnev would go on to justify the invasion in the months afterwards in what became known as the 'Brezhnev Doctrine'. According to this doctrine, the USSR had the right to invade any country in Eastern Europe whose actions appeared to threaten the security of the whole Eastern Bloc. Brezhnev argued that Dubcek's actions had threatened to undermine the Warsaw Pact and communist control in Eastern Europe, and therefore the Soviet Union had to invade.

The Soviet invasion of Czechoslovakia

Soviet tanks rolled into Czechoslovakia on the evening of 20 August 1968. Dubcek ordered the Czech people not to respond with violence. Nonetheless, there was a great deal of non-violent civil disobedience. For example, many students stood in the way of tanks holding anti-invasion banners.

Dubcek was arrested and taken to Moscow where Brezhnev tearfully told him that he had betrayed socialism. Dubcek was forced to sign the Moscow Protocol, which committed the Czech government to 'protect socialism' by reintroducing censorship and removing political opposition.

People in Prague on 21 August 1968, holding up the Czechoslovakian flag and throwing burning torches in an attempt to stop a Soviet tank.

Exam-style question

Describe the key features of the Brezhnev Doctrine. **(6 marks)**

Activity

Imagine you are a reporter working in Moscow in 1968. You must prepare a telegram to send back to your newspaper in London explaining what the Brezhnev Doctrine is and why it has been introduced.

Each word of a telegram costs money, so you need to summarise this information in as few words as possible. However, you mustn't miss out any key pieces of information.

Write your telegram, trying to use as few words as possible. Compare your telegram to that of the person next to you. Have they used fewer words than you? Have they covered all of the key points? Together, produce another version of the telegram, trying to reduce your word count even further.

Czechoslovakia: international reaction

Learning objectives

In this chapter you will learn about:

- America's reaction to the Soviet invasion of Czechoslovakia
- the divisions in European communism created by the invasion.

America's response

Brezhnev believed that America would do nothing to help the Czechoslovakian people. America was already fighting a bloody war against communism in Vietnam. Brezhnev was confident that America wanted to avoid a further military entanglement. Therefore, while America publicly condemned the invasion, it offered no military support against it.

Western European response

Western European governments followed America's lead – they condemned the invasion but provided no military help. The reaction of Western European Communist Parties was more surprising. Communist Parties in Italy and France, for example, were outraged by the Soviet invasion. Therefore, they formally declared themselves independent of the Soviet Communist Party. This created rival forms of European communism – Soviet communism in the East, and Eurocommunism in the West. This was very important because it showed the extent to which Soviet communism had lost authority and support as a result of the invasion.

Eastern European response

The Soviet invasion also led to discontent in Eastern Europe. Significantly, the Yugoslavian and Romanian governments both condemned the invasion and distanced themselves from the Soviet Union. Following 1968, Yugoslavian and Romanian communists formed alliances with China, the world's other major communist power, further dividing the communist world. However, the East German and Polish governments welcomed the Soviet response – as they were concerned that Czechoslovakia was being too liberal. These pro-Moscow leaders might lose their jobs if Czech reforms were allowed to spread to other Eastern Bloc countries.

examzone

Top tip

Timing is very important in the exam. Before you start writing, make a brief note of the timings for each question. We suggest spending roughly:

- 3 minutes on Question 1
- 7 minutes on Question 2
- 15 minutes on Question 3
- 9 minutes on Question 4
- 22 minutes on Question 5
- 19 minutes on Question 6

If you qualify for extra time, remember to include this when you work out your timings.

The Czech people demonstrate against the Russian presence in Prague.

examzone
Build better answers

Exam question: Explain why relations between the Soviet Union and the USA changed in the years 1957–69. (13 marks)

You may use the following in your answer.
- The Cuban Missile Crisis
- Disagreements over the future of Berlin.

You must also include information of your own. You need to make relevant points, supported by specific examples, with a clear focus on how each factor led to the situation described.

In each level, the number of statements you make will affect the quality of your answer. For example, in level 2, a single developed argument is unlikely to provide as complete an answer as three developed arguments.

■ **A basic answer (level 1)** is correct, but does not have details to support it (for example, *One reason why the relationship between the Soviet Union and the USA changed was because of the Cuban Missile Crisis*).

● **A good answer (level 2)** provides the details as well but does not explain how they caused the event process mentioned in the question (for example, *One reason why the relationship between the Soviet Union and the USA changed was because of the Cuban Missile Crisis). Following the Cuban Missile Crisis, the USA and USSR negotiated a Test Ban Treaty (August 1963), which banned all nuclear tests except those carried out underground.*).

▲ **A better answer (level 3)** provides reasons, supports these with detail and explains how they caused the event process mentioned in the question (for example, *One reason why the relationship between the Soviet Union and the USA changed was because of the Cuban Missile Crisis. Following the Cuban Missile Crisis, the USA and USSR negotiated a Test Ban Treaty (August 1963), which banned all nuclear tests except those carried out underground. This changed the relationship between the Soviet Union and the USA because this was the first time since the beginning of the Cold War that the two superpowers had tried to limit the arms race. Before this, the arms race was very competitive and there was a continuous threat of nuclear war*).

▲ **An excellent answer (level 4)** shows how the reasons are linked and/or reaches a judgement about their relative importance.

Make sure you write accurately – there are 3 extra marks available for spelling, grammar and punctuation in these questions.

Now write another paragraph in answer to this question. Choose one of the points mentioned below, add examples and explain how this factor is linked to the factor discussed above and reach a judgement about which of the two factors is most important.
- Disagreements over the future of Berlin
- The creation of the Washington-Moscow hotline
- The effects of the Soviet invasion of Czechoslovakia.

Activity

Complete the speech bubbles below to show the different reactions to the Soviet invasion of Czechoslovakia.

Lyndon B. Johnson, president of the USA.

Josip Broz Tito, communist leader of Yugoslavia.

Jacques Duclos, leader of the French communists.

Key Topic 3: Why did the Cold War end?

Following the Cuban Missile Crisis, relations between the two superpowers mellowed, leading to a period of relative stability and peace. However, good relations were undermined by the Soviet invasion of Afghanistan and the election of a new American president who believed that the Cold War was a moral mission: a fight between good and evil. As a result, the 1980s witnessed renewed hostility between the superpowers during an era known as the Second Cold War.

In this section you will study:

- détente and its collapse
- President Reagan and the 'Second Cold War'
- Premier Gorbachev, the fall of the Berlin Wall, and the collapse of the Soviet Union.

You will consider the reasons why both superpowers sought détente, a period of relative peace in the Cold War. You will also consider the achievements of détente and how the Soviet invasion of Afghanistan led to a breakdown in the relationship between the USA and the USSR. You will also study the impact of the last two 'Cold War Warriors': US President Ronald Reagan and Russian Premier Mikhail Gorbachev. Finally, you will examine the reasons for the end of the Cold War and the collapse of the Soviet Union.

Détente – the search for peace

Learning objectives

In this chapter you will learn about:

● the treaties in 1967 and 1968 which began détente

● the SALT 1 Treaty, negotiations for the SALT 2 Treaty, the Apollo-Soyuz mission, and the Helsinki Conference.

The Cuban Missile Crisis of 1962 brought the world to the brink of a nuclear holocaust. During the late 1960s and 1970s, Soviet and American leaders tried to ease the tensions in their relationship. In the West, this policy was known by the French word *détente*; the Russians called it *razryadka*. Russia and America signed two important treaties at the end of the 1960s that are good examples of the détente relationship. The treaties were important because they limited the possibility of further conflict between the superpowers.

● The 1967 Outer Space Treaty stopped the arms race spreading to outer space as it pledged that no nuclear weapons would be placed in space by either superpower.

● The 1968 Nuclear Non-Proliferation Treaty agreed that neither superpower would supply nuclear weapons to other states or help other states to develop nuclear weapons. This stopped superpower conflict engulfing other areas of the world.

The high point of détente was reached in the mid-1970s, with three important statements of the new understanding between the two superpowers.

The SALT 1 Treaty and negotiations for the SALT 2 Treaty

The Strategic Arms Limitation Treaty (SALT 1), 1972 imposed limits on the nuclear capability of Russia and the USA.

● The USA and USSR agreed that there would be no further production of strategic ballistic missiles (short-range, lightweight missiles).

● Both powers agreed that submarines carrying nuclear weapons would only be introduced when existing stocks of intercontinental ballistic missiles became obsolete.

● The ABM (Anti-Ballistic Missile) Treaty was agreed. If developed, ABMs could shoot down incoming nuclear missiles. If one side achieved this first, it would effectively give them a dangerous edge in the arms race. Both sides were limited to two ABM systems each.

SALT 1 was signed by the American president and the Soviet premier in 1972. It was significant because it was the first agreement between the superpowers that successfully limited the number of nuclear weapons they held. It also showed that détente had created an environment in which the two sides could co-operate on important issues.

Exam-style question

Explain the importance of three of the following in international relations. **(15 marks)**

● Détente
● SALT treaties
● Helsinki Conference
● Apollo-Soyuz mission

The Origins of SALT 2

SALT 1 was intended to be a temporary agreement leading to a more comprehensive treaty. Consequently, negotiations for SALT 2 began in 1972. The negotiations were difficult for two main reasons:

- The West German government was worried that further arms reductions would leave their territory undefended.
- Right-wing American Congressmen thought that détente had gone too far and were reluctant to agree to further compromises with the Soviet Union.

Nonetheless, in 1974, the Vladivostok Agreement, part of the SALT 2 negotiations, set out an important principle: both sides agreed to reduce their stocks of nuclear warheads to 2250.

SALT 2 was eventually signed by US President Carter and Soviet Premier Brezhnev in June 1979.

Astronauts from the Apollo–Soyuz mission, 1975. The two crews sit in front of their flags. In front of the two crews is a model showing the docking of the two spacecraft.

The Apollo-Soyuz Mission

In 1975 a joint space mission was launched in which an American Apollo spacecraft and a Russian Soyuz spacecraft docked high above the Earth. The 1960s had been dominated by an extremely competitive race to the moon, but this marked the beginning of superpower co-operation in space.

The Helsinki Agreements, 1975

The Helsinki Conference had representatives from 35 countries. They came from all of Europe, except Andorra and Albania. There were also representatives from the USSR, the USA and Canada. They discussed an agreement that had taken two years to draft. The terms of the agreement applied to everyone. There were three main issues: security, co-operation and human rights.

Security

- All country boundaries were accepted (so East and West Germany accepted each other's existence for the first time).
- All disputes were to be settled peacefully (if necessary through the UN), not by use of threats or force.
- No country would interfere in the internal affairs of another country.
- Countries would inform each other about any big military manoeuvres and would accept representatives from other countries to observe them.

Co-operation

Countries agreed to co-operate on many different levels. For example:

- economic co-operation through trade (so the USA would buy oil from the USSR, whilst the USSR would buy wheat from the USA)
- industrial co-operation through setting the same standards and running joint industrial projects
- scientific co-operation through sharing information and research (for example, in medicine or space research)
- educational co-operation (for example, learning languages, student exchanges).

Human Rights

Countries should respect human rights, including:

- freedom of speech
- freedom of movement
- freedom of religion
- freedom of information.

The Helsinki Agreements stabilised the situation in Europe by agreeing greater co-operation between the superpowers and their European allies in terms of trade and fighting international terrorism. This limited the possibility of superpower conflict by creating a stable relationship between the USSR and America in Europe.

Activity

In groups choose one of these five key events of the détente period:

- Outer Space Treaty
- Nuclear Non-Proliferation Treaty
- SALT 1
- Helsinki Conference
- Apollo–Soyuz mission.

Imagine it is the time of this event. Present a news report to the rest of the class explaining what has happened and why it is important.

The collapse of détente: the Soviet invasion of Afghanistan

Learning objectives

In this chapter you will learn about:
- the Kabul Revolution
- the establishment of a communist regime in Afghanistan
- the reasons for the Soviet invasion of Afghanistan.

The Kabul Revolution: April 1978

Even détente could not stop superpower competition over the developing world. Indeed, Soviet leader Brezhnev saw the communist revolution in Afghanistan as an opportunity to extend his power in the oil-rich Middle East. The Kabul Revolution of April 1978 witnessed the dramatic overthrow of the government. The new government, based in the Afghan capital of Kabul, was determined 'to build socialism in Afghanistan'. The new communist president, Mohammed Taraki, quickly became an ally of the USSR.

However, the revolutionary government of Afghanistan was far from stable. It suffered from personal rivalries and disagreements. Moreover, many Muslim leaders across the country were angered by the socialist reforms the government introduced. By the spring of 1979 this anger had caused a civil war to break out across the country between government and Islamic fighters. President Taraki was forced to accept Hafizullah Amin, the head of the army, as prime minister. But the two men quickly became bitter rivals. In October 1979, Amin supporters assassinated Taraki and Amin claimed presidency of the country.

The Soviet invasion: December 1979

Following Amin's seizure of power, Brezhnev ordered the Soviet invasion of Afghanistan. Brezhnev took the decision for the following reasons.

- Although Amin was a communist, the USSR did not trust him. The Soviet secret police reported that he was an American spy. He was also unpopular with a large number of Muslims in the country and Brezhnev feared that Muslim groups were planning to take control of the country.
- The USSR was concerned that, as a result of the civil war, Afghanistan would become an Islamic state and influence nearby Soviet republics to do the same. The Islamic states were not communist and therefore any countries that became Islamic would have no reason to make alliances with Russia.
- Babrak Karmal, an Afghani communist, argued that he had enough popular support to form a new government but needed Soviet help to defeat Amin's military.
- Brezhnev believed that America would tolerate the invasion, as it had done in Czechoslovakia following the 'Prague Spring' to avoid war.

Soviet troops killed Amin along with many of his supporters, and Karmal was declared president (a post he retained until 1986). Yet the invasion proved to be a disaster both for Afghanistan and the Soviet Union. It lasted ten years and around 1.5 million people died, including almost 15,000 Russian soldiers.

examzone
Build better answers

Exam question: Outline two reasons why the Soviet Union invaded Afghanistan in 1979.   (4 marks)
You need to make two developed statements. These are statements that answer the question and provide some additional detail.

■ A basic answer

Brezhnev ordered the invasion of Afghanistan because he believed that Hafizullah Amin, the new president, was an American spy. Russian intelligence reports suggested that Amin was trying to do a deal with America.

● A good answer

Brezhnev ordered the invasion of Afghanistan because he believed that Hafizullah Amin, the new president, was an American spy. Russian intelligence reports suggested that Amin was trying to do a deal with America. Another reason why Brezhnev ordered the invasion of Afghanistan was because he was worried that Afghanistan would become an Islamic state. Brezhnev knew that Islamic states did not share the Soviet Union's communist ideology and therefore would have no reason to make an alliance with Russia.

Activities

The Soviet invasion of Afghanistan might seem to be a quite complicated topic. You must produce *A Beginner's Guide to the Soviet Invasion of Afghanistan* so that people can understand this important event.

1 Copy the table below.

A Beginner's Guide to the Soviet Invasion of Afghanistan

Who?	What?	Why?

2 Now add relevant information in each column.

- In the first column, list the key people mentioned in this chapter and provide brief details about their role – you may choose to find pictures to illustrate this part of your guide.

- In the second column, describe the key events of the invasion. (The second column below has been started for you as an example.)

- In the final column, explain in your own words the reason why the invasion was launched – you may choose to do this as a diagram.

A Beginner's Guide to the Soviet Invasion of Afghanistan

Who?	What?	Why?
	In December 1979, Brezhnev ordered Soviet troops to invade Afghanistan. The war that followed this invasion lasted ten years and 1.5 million people were killed.	

The collapse of détente: the American reaction to the Soviet invasion of Afghanistan

> ## Learning objectives
>
> In this chapter you will learn about:
> - President Carter's immediate reaction to the invasion of Afghanistan
> - the failure of the SALT 2 Treaty
> - the American boycott of the Moscow Olympic Games.

The Carter Doctrine

Brezhnev's invasion was a severe miscalculation. The American president, Jimmy Carter, was appalled at the Soviet aggression. Consequently, he made a statement that became known as the Carter Doctrine. Essentially, he argued that the USA would not allow the USSR to gain control of territory in the oil-rich Middle East. He also immediately took a number of steps to try to remove Soviet troops from Afghanistan.

US President Jimmy Carter and Soviet leader Leonid Brezhnev arrive outside the Soviet Embassy in Vienna, Austria, for the SALT 2 Treaty talks, June 1979.

1 He formed an alliance with China and Israel to support Afghan rebels, who were opposed to the Soviet invasion and the Afghan communist government. America's Central Intelligence Agency (CIA) provided weapons and funds for the Mujahideen – an Islamic organisation which was fighting to free Afghanistan from Soviet control.

2 He imposed **economic sanctions** (restrictions), stopping virtually all trade with the Soviet Union.

3 He ended diplomatic relations with the Soviet Union.

The end of détente

Carter's actions did not force Soviet troops to withdraw from Afghanistan. However, they did effectively end détente. Indeed, Carter took two further steps that showed that détente was over.

The end of SALT 2

Carter had signed the SALT 2 treaty in June 1979. However, in response to the Soviet invasion of Afghanistan the US Senate refused to ratify the treaty and therefore it never became law.

Increased defence spending

At the same time Carter increased US defence spending by 5 per cent. In addition Carter ordered the US military to come up with plans for surviving and winning a nuclear war with the Soviet Union. These measures indicated that he was taking a more hard-line approach to superpower relations.

The Olympic boycott

Additionally, Carter led a boycott of the 1980 Moscow Olympic Games. Around sixty countries, including China, Malawi, West Germany and Zaire, followed the American lead and refused to attend the games in protest at the Soviet invasion of Afghanistan. The American government set up an alternative Olympics, called the Olympic Boycott Games, which was held in Philadelphia. The American press ridiculed the official Olympic Games and nicknamed Misha Bear, Russia's Olympic mascot, Gulag Bear – a reference to Soviet prison camps, which were known as *gulags*.

The 1984 Los Angeles Olympic Games was also highly political. In retaliation for the 1980 boycott, the USSR and 14 communist countries refused to attend the Los Angeles Olympic Games. The USSR organised the Friendship Games as a communist alternative.

By 1980 détente was dead. The invasion of Afghanistan and the American response meant that superpower relations were at their lowest point since the Cuban Missile Crisis of 1962.

Did you know?

During the 1984 Los Angeles Olympic Games, McDonalds ran a campaign called 'When the US Wins, You Win'. Customers were offered free food every time America won a medal: a Coca-Cola for a bronze medal, fries for a silver medal and a Big Mac for a gold medal. The campaign was a financial disaster for McDonalds, as the Soviet boycott of the Olympics led to many more American medals than expected.

examzone
Build better answers

Exam question: Describe one factor that led to the end of détente. (2 marks)

■ **A basic answer (level 1)** is accurate but lacks detail.

● **A good answer (level 2)** is accurate and includes supporting information.

Look at the question above. Take one of the following factors:
- the Soviet invasion of Afghanistan
- the Carter Doctrine
- American withdrawal from the SALT 2 negotiations.

What supporting information would you use to develop your point?

Activity

Imagine you are part of the committee organising the Olympic Boycott Games in Philadelphia in 1980. You must design a mascot for these Olympics. The mascot should in some way represent the values that President Carter was defending when he chose to boycott the Moscow Olympic Games. Draw a picture of your mascot and label the key features, linking them to the reasons for the boycott.

Reagan and the 'Second Cold War': 'Evil Empire'

> **Learning objectives**
>
> In this chapter you will learn about:
> - what is meant by the 'Second Cold War'
> - President Reagan's attitude to the Cold War
> - the 'Evil Empire' speech.

The 'Second Cold War'

The 'Second Cold War' is a phrase used to describe the period between 1979 and 1985, which marked a new low in superpower relations. As in the late 1950s and early 1960s, the public was extremely concerned about the possibility of nuclear war. This anxiety was reflected in popular culture, particularly in television shows such as the American TV movie *The Day After* (1983) and the British TV drama *Threads* (1984).

President Reagan

Détente had fallen apart under President Carter. Ronald Reagan, who became the new American president in 1981, had no intention of putting it back together. Indeed, he believed it was time for America to start fighting again: Reagan wanted to win the Cold War.

The American media were not convinced that Reagan was suitable to be president. He was famous for starring in low-budget 1950s movies. His most famous role was in the film *Bedtime for Bonzo* (1951), in which he starred alongside a chimp. Reagan was portrayed as a modern-day cowboy, who knew nothing of world affairs and was totally unqualified to be American president. French and British commentators were also worried by Reagan, particularly when he stated that he could imagine 'a limited nuclear war in Europe'.

Nonetheless, Reagan had strong ideas on the future of the Cold War. For example, he believed that détente had been a disaster for the USA. He thought the policy had made the USA weak while allowing the USSR to grow strong. Reagan rejected the idea of peaceful co-existence with the USSR, believing that it was America's destiny to fight for individual freedom in the Cold War.

'Evil Empire'

Reagan made his view of the Soviet Union plain in his famous 'Evil Empire' speech in March 1983. Reagan was a committed Christian and gave this speech at a meeting of the National Association of Evangelicals, a Christian organisation. Reagan argued that the Cold War was a fight between good and evil, and that America fought with God's blessing.

Reagan urged Americans not to: 'ignore the facts of history and the aggressive impulses of an evil empire' and to 'remove yourself from the struggle between right and wrong and good and evil'. Reagan's point was that the Cold War was a moral war and that America had a moral duty to invest in new nuclear weapons in order to defend liberty from the 'evil' Soviet Union.

> A number of years ago, I heard a young father give a speech in which he said, 'I love my little girls more than anything'. He went on: 'I would rather see my little girls die now; still believing in God, than have them grow up under communism and one day die no longer believing in God'. There were thousands of young people in that audience. They came to their feet with shouts of joy. They had instantly recognised the profound truth in what he had said.

Source A: *An extract from President Reagan's 'Evil Empire' speech given in March 1983. Adapted from www.americanrhetoric.com/speeches/ ronaldreaganevilempire.htm*

EUROPE

U.S.A

ZOKE

"I CAN ENVISAGE A LIMITED NUCLEAR WAR IN EUROPE"—REAGAN

Source B: *This cartoon appeared in the Sun newspaper on 21 October 1981. Reagan is dressed as a cowboy in the foreground, while Brezhnev is the figure in the background. Both are trying to destroy Europe.*

Did you know?

In the 1980s, the British government had a plan for surviving a nuclear war. The British army would surround all the cities that were bombed to ensure that survivors could not leave. The government worked out that the survivors in the cities would die within two weeks due to radiation sickness. They believed that they would cause fewer problems if they all died in one place rather than escaping to the countryside.

examzone
Build better answers

Exam Question: How useful are Sources A and B as evidence of the reasons for Reagan's hard-line attitude to the Soviet Union? Explain your answer using Sources A and B and your own knowledge.
(10 marks)

■ **A basic answer (level 1)** makes simple comments on the content or provenance of the sources.

● **A good answer (level 2)** reaches a judgement about the usefulness of the sources based on their content or origin.

▲ **An excellent answer (level 3)** reaches a judgement about the usefulness of the sources based on their content and origin and linking this to the purpose stated in the question.

Activity

Imagine you are a freelance journalist writing for newspapers in the United Kingdom. It is the day after Reagan's 'Evil Empire' speech. You have been asked by two newspapers to write a report on the speech.

The first newspaper requires a balanced report on the speech. Your report must explain what was said in the speech and why this is important in the context of the Cold War. It must not reveal your opinion about the speech.

The second newspaper requires a highly opinionated report on the speech. You must state clearly if you agree or disagree with Reagan's opinion, and you must explain how the speech has changed your opinion of President Reagan.

You may choose to use the text from Reagan's speech in either or both of your reports.

Reagan and the 'Second Cold War': 'Star Wars' – America strikes back

Learning objectives

In this chapter you will learn about:

- Reagan's vision of SDI
- the problems created by SDI
- the shift in the arms race.

Reagan's vision

Many of Reagan's closest advisors misunderstood him. They thought that when he talked about victory in the Cold War, he was only trying to win support from the American people. But Reagan had a bold vision: he was determined to win the Cold War. He honestly believed that the USA should fight to win. Specifically, Reagan believed that the USSR could be forced to disarm by his new initiative: SDI (Strategic Defence Initiative).

SDI – 'Star Wars'

Reagan's plan for winning the Cold War involved taking the arms race to a new level. He proposed a 'nuclear umbrella', which would stop Soviet nuclear bombs from reaching American soil. Reagan's plan was to launch an army of satellites equipped with powerful lasers, which would intercept Soviet missiles in space and destroy them before they could do America any harm. For obvious reasons, Reagan's scheme soon became known as 'Star Wars'. Reagan believed that his 'Star Wars' technology would make Soviet nuclear missiles useless and therefore force the USSR to disarm.

SDI was a turning point in the arms race. During détente, the superpowers had been evenly matched and had worked together to limit the growth of their nuclear stockpiles. SDI was a complete break from this policy. In fact, SDI broke the terms of the Outer Space Treaty of 1967 (see page 47), which was signed during détente and had committed the superpowers to use space technology for peace alone.

examzone
Top tip

Structure is really important when answering a question such as the one on page 57 (about how SDI affected the superpowers' relationship). Rather than writing everything you know, break down your answer into three key points. Ensure that you back up each point with examples before moving on to the next point.

The Soviet response to SDI

SDI presented enormous problems for the Russians. Soviet leaders knew perfectly well that they could not compete with Reagan's 'Star Wars' plan.

First, America had won the race to the moon in 1969, and by the early 1980s it had developed the next generation of spacecraft: the space shuttle.

Secondly, the Soviet economy was not producing enough wealth to fund consumer goods, conventional military spending and the development of new space-based weapons.

Finally, the USSR was behind America in terms of its computer technology. During the 1980s, the American computer market boomed. Prior to the SDI, however, Soviet leaders were highly suspicious of computers because they were concerned they might be used to undermine the power of the Communist Party. For example, computers with word processors and printers could be used to produce anti-government propaganda, or computers linked to telephones could be used to leak secrets to governments in the West. Computers were essential for the development of a 'Star Wars'-type programme.

For these reasons, Reagan's proposals meant that the USSR could no longer compete in the arms race.

Activity

In the exam, it is important that you support your general points with specific examples. Complete the following spider diagram by adding specific examples from this chapter.

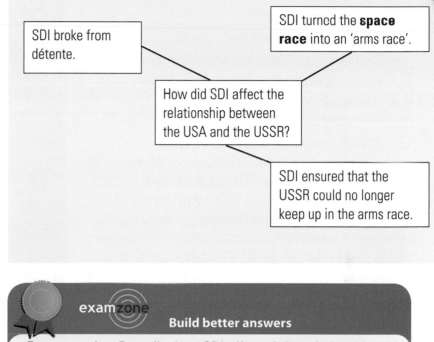

SDI broke from détente.

SDI turned the **space race** into an 'arms race'.

How did SDI affect the relationship between the USA and the USSR?

SDI ensured that the USSR could no longer keep up in the arms race.

examzone
Build better answers

Exam question: Describe how SDI affected the relationship between the USA and the USSR.   (6 marks)

■ **A basic answer (level 1)** contains simple statements that are accurate but contain no supporting examples.

● **A good answer (level 2)** contains statements that are accurate and are developed with specific information.

▲ **An excellent answer (full marks)** includes two or three detailed statements. Each statement must make a relevant point, backed up with specific examples and an explanation of how this affected the relationship between the USA and the USSR.

For the question above, you can use the notes you made on your spider diagram. How would you develop and explain the following effects of SDI?
• SDI broke from détente.
• SDI turned the space race into an arms race.
• SDI ensured that the USSR could no longer keep up in the arms race.

Gorbachev and the end of the Cold War: 'new thinking' in Russia

> ### Learning objectives
>
> In this chapter you will learn about:
> - Gorbachev's vision for communism
> - Gorbachev's relationship with the West
> - Gorbachev's 'new thinking'.

Gorbachev and communism

Mikhail Gorbachev was the last leader of the Soviet Union, serving from 1985 until its collapse in 1991. He oversaw the end of the Cold War, the fall of the Berlin Wall and the end of communism in Russia. However, it was never his intention to undermine communism. Rather, he hoped to be communism's saviour.

Gorbachev's relationship with the West

Gorbachev had very little foreign policy experience prior to becoming the leader of Russia. At first, he viewed the relationship with America in rather simplistic terms. For example, following his first meeting with President Reagan in 1985, he commented that 'Reagan is not just a class enemy; he is extremely primitive. He looks like a caveman and is mentally retarded.'

Gorbachev's relationship with the West was tested over the Chernobyl crisis. In April 1986, the nuclear reactor in the Chernobyl nuclear power plant in the Ukraine went critical and exploded. Initially, Gorbachev authorised a cover story that denied there had been a release of dangerous radiation. The Western media were unconvinced by the Soviet cover story and Western governments put pressure on Gorbachev to tell the truth about the scale of the disaster. Chernobyl became an international symbol of the crisis in Soviet communism.

The Chernobyl nuclear power plant after it exploded in April 1986.

Gorbachev's 'new thinking'

Gorbachev himself recognised that communism in Russia faced many problems.

- The Soviet economy was not nearly as efficient as the American economy. While Americans in the 1980s enjoyed an excellent standard of living, everyday life in Russia was dominated by shortages. For example, it was not uncommon for housewives in Moscow to queue for up to five hours simply to get a packet of sausages.
- Many of the Soviet people had lost faith in the Communist Party.

Gorbachev's plan for reviving communism involved a radical programme of reform. This was often summarised in two words:

- *perestroika* (restructuring) – economic reforms designed to make the Soviet economy more efficient
- *glasnost* (openness) – censorship of the press was to be relaxed.

Gorbachev assumed that *perestroika* and *glasnost* would strengthen the power of the Soviet Communist Party. Indeed, although Gorbachev talked about reform, he was very slow to allow democratic elections in Russia.

> The main reason for Gorbachev's popularity was the visible signs that Russia was changing. He made it possible to buy Western newspapers and magazines; the cloak of government secrecy was slowly lifted; and the press began publishing sensational articles on Stalin and past Soviet leaders. He enabled the people to gain a sense of themselves as individuals, and in so doing he accelerated the decline of the Soviet system.

Adapted from Dimitri Volkogonov, *The Rise and Fall of the Soviet Empire*, 1999.

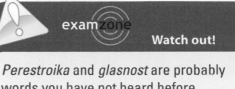

Watch out!

Perestroika and *glasnost* are probably words you have not heard before. Try not to get their definitions confused. For example, think about the similar sounds of 'stroika' and 'structure' to remember that *perestroika* means restructuring.

Activities

1 Copy the following cards describing some of Gorbachev's early attitudes and measures.

Wanted to save communism	Stayed silent over Chernobyl	Talked about democracy
Launched glasnost	Had very little foreign policy experience	Recognised the need to reform the USSR
Launched perestroika	Took a long time to hold democratic elections in Russia	Thought Reagan was a class enemy

2 On a large sheet of paper, draw the following scale.

Strengthened relationships with the West ———————— Weakened relationships with the West

Read each card. Decide how this factor changed Russia's relationship with the West. Place each card in an appropriate place on the scale.

3 Use your completed scale to write a paragraph in answer to the following: *Describe how Gorbachev's early attitudes and measures strengthened Russia's relationship with the West.*

Gorbachev and the end of the Cold War: Reagan and Gorbachev's changing relationship

> ### Learning objectives
>
> In this chapter you will learn about:
> - the strengths and weaknesses of the superpowers in 1985
> - three summits and the INF Treaty
> - the reasons for the changing relationship between the USA and the USSR.

The positions of the superpowers in 1986

When Gorbachev became leader of Russia in 1985, it was clear that the USA was in a much stronger position than the USSR.

	USA	USSR
Strengths	<ul><li>booming economy</li><li>excellent computer technology</li><li>excellent space technology</li><li>highly equipped conventional military forces</li><li>international reputation as 'leaders of the free world'</li><li>NATO allies</li></ul>	<ul><li>Warsaw Pact allies</li><li>greater number of nuclear missiles than the USA</li></ul>
Weaknesses	<ul><li>fewer nuclear missiles than the USSR</li></ul>	<ul><li>committed to an expensive war in Afghanistan</li><li>failing economy</li><li>old-fashioned technology</li><li>reputation ruined by the Chernobyl crisis</li></ul>

Geneva and Reykjavik

The first meeting between President Reagan and Premier Gorbachev occurred at the Geneva Summit in November 1985. Reagan was clearly in the stronger position. Nonetheless, his aims were fairly limited.

Reagan's aim for the conference was to persuade Gorbachev that he sincerely desired peace between the two superpowers. Gorbachev, although in a weaker position, was hoping to persuade Reagan to drop his plans for SDI.

Gorbachev was also keen to establish a working relationship with the American president. Indeed, prior to the meeting, he sacked the long-serving Soviet foreign minister, Andrei Gromyko, and appointed Eduard Shevardnadze as his replacement. This move signalled an end to the aggressive foreign policy that had been pursued by Gromyko.

The Geneva meeting was significant because the two leaders were able to talk face-to-face and develop a personal relationship. However, no formal agreement on arms control was reached.

The Reykjavik meeting of October 1986 was much more ambitious. Reagan proposed scrapping all **ballistic nuclear missiles**. Gorbachev, however, was unwilling to agree to these proposals because Reagan refused to drop his SDI project.

Reagan and conciliation

Why did Reagan later change his mind about the USSR to the extent of wanting to resume détente with the 'Evil Empire'? Several things changed his mind.

- He could see public opinion was against another arms race. He wanted to save the money that an arms race would cost the USA. He also did not want the USA to be seen as a brutal bully. There had been large-scale demonstrations across Western Europe against the siting of US missiles there. In 1984, before Gorbachev came to power, Reagan had stopped using phrases such as 'Evil Empire' and begun to use phrases such as 'mutual compromise' and calling 1984 'a year of opportunity for peace'.

- He could see there was widespread approval of Gorbachev and his changes in the USSR. There was such enthusiasm for Gorbachev's reforms that a new word was invented to describe it: 'Gorbymania'. This spread from the USSR through the Eastern European states to many other countries, including the USA. Gorbachev was the first ruler of the USSR to gain significant public approval in the USA. He had also won the approval of other heads of state, including the British prime minister, Margaret Thatcher.

- He got on with Gorbachev and seems to have believed that Gorbachev wanted reforms in the USSR and an end to the Cold War. Once Reagan had decided to try for détente, he made sure that he got the publicity right. For example, when he and Gorbachev met, he made sure that they, and their wives, looked as if they genuinely got on.

INF Treaty

Following the Reykjavik meeting, American and Soviet diplomats continued to try to draft an arms-reduction treaty. The result was the Intermediate-Range Nuclear Forces (INF) Treaty, signed in Washington in December 1987. The treaty eliminated all nuclear missiles with a range of 500–5500 kilometres (310–3400 miles).

The INF Treaty was significant because it was the first treaty to reduce the number of nuclear missiles that the superpowers possessed. It therefore went much further than SALT 1, which simply limited the growth of Russian and American nuclear stockpiles. During the next four years, the two sides destroyed hundreds of missiles and strict procedures were put in place to task inspectors to ensure the treaty was followed. It was a great breakthrough.

Premier Gorbachev (sitting on the left) and President Reagan sign the INF Treaty, Washington, December 1987.

Why did Gorbachev sign the INF Treaty?

Gorbachev had refused to agree to an arms treaty in Reykjavik because Reagan refused to drop his plans for SDI. Nonetheless, a year later he signed the INF Treaty in spite of the fact that Reagan was still committed to SDI. Why did Gorbachev change his mind?

- Gorbachev came to see that nuclear weapons were highly expensive but added nothing to Soviet security.
- Reagan persuaded Gorbachev that the USA had no intention of invading the USSR.
- Gorbachev realised that the Soviet economy could never recover as long as it was spending so much money on nuclear weapons.
- Gorbachev believed that disarmament would win him popularity in the West and that this would allow him to make profitable trade deals between the USSR and the West.
- Gorbachev believed that political and economic measures would be more effective in guaranteeing Russia's security than military strength.

Summit conferences after Reagan

In 1988, Ronald Reagan went to Moscow for the first time for a summit conference. They agreed to work towards disarmament of both nuclear and conventional arms. The summit fixed no targets, but it eased the tensions created by Afghanistan and opened the way to the agreements that took place after Reagan left the presidency.

The Malta Summit, 1989

The summit was a meeting between US President George Bush and President Gorbachev. This meeting began work on the agreements that were to be CFE (1990) and START I (1991), below.

The CFE Agreement, 1990

This agreement, signed by Bush and Gorbachev, set limits to the non-nuclear forces that the Warsaw Pact and NATO could have in Europe. Negotiations for this began in 1989 and the process was made difficult because the USSR was beginning to break up at the time. This meant that, for example, Hungary was part of the Warsaw Pact when negotiations began, but had left by the time the Treaty was ready to be signed.

START I, 1991

Signed by Bush and Gorbachev, with pens made from scrapped nuclear missiles, this set limits to the numbers of nuclear weapons. Both sides agreed to reduce their holdings of nuclear warheads by about a third, by destroying them. It also agreed that both sides would continue to reduce. It did not agree on all kinds of nuclear weapons (the agreement did not cover some nuclear submarines or space weapons), but covered most of them.

Activities

1 Use the information in this chapter to complete the following table.

Summit	Gorbachev's aims	Degree of success for Gorbachev	Reagan's aims	Degree of success for Reagan
Geneva				
Reykjavik				
Washington				

2 Choose one of the summits. Imagine you are either Premier Gorbachev or President Reagan. Write a brief note to your advisors explaining what has been achieved at the summit and how you feel about the outcome of the meeting.

Gorbachev and the end of the Cold War: the break-up of Eastern Europe and the fall of the Berlin Wall

> ### Learning objectives
>
> In this chapter you will learn about:
> - Gorbachev's attitude to Eastern Europe
> - the loosening Soviet grip on Eastern Europe
> - the fall of the Berlin Wall and the end of the Warsaw Pact.

Gorbachev's attitude to Eastern Europe

Gorbachev's attitude to Eastern Europe can be summarised in the following way:

- In December 1988, he announced that ideology should play a smaller role in Soviet foreign affairs. In practice, this meant that the USSR would no longer favour trade with communist states over trade with capitalist countries.
- Gorbachev was keen for Eastern European states to enjoy *perestroika* and *glasnost*.
- Gorbachev withdrew Soviet troops from Eastern European bases in order to save money.

The break-up of the Eastern Bloc

Gorbachev had never intended to weaken communist control of Eastern Europe. Once again, his desire was to strengthen communism by reform. However, once reform had started in the Eastern Bloc, he was unable to contain it. The Eastern Bloc had previously relied on the Soviet army to prop up their pro-Moscow regimes. There would not be another invasion of Hungary or Czechoslovakia, so the Eastern European governments were weakened.

Germany: East Germans leave for West Germany via Hungary. Communist Party of East Germany declares free elections. Berlin Wall falls in November 1989. Communists defeated in 1990 elections.

Poland: Communist government defeated in free elections held in June 1989.

Czech Republic / Slovakia: Popular protests lead to the overthrow of communist rule in the 'Velvet Revolution' of November 1989.

Hungary: The communist government promises a new democratic constitution in summer 1989, and the first free elections are held in spring 1989.

A German celebrates the fall of the Berlin Wall, 12 November 1989. There were days of jubilant celebrations at the uniting of East and West Berlin.

The fall of the Berlin Wall

The fall of the Berlin Wall has come to symbolise the end of the Cold War. However, it would be wrong to confuse the fall of the wall with the end of the war.

The fall of the Berlin Wall is an excellent case study of the effects of reform in Eastern Europe. East Germany was slow to embrace *perestroika* and *glasnost*. Indeed, the East German government even banned Russian publications during the 1980s because they were too liberal. However, the communist government was unable to contain its citizens' desire for freedom once neighbouring states had abandoned communism.

As soon as democratic elections were announced in Hungary there was a mass movement of East German citizens through Hungary to West Germany. As a result, the East German government was forced to announce much greater freedom of travel for East German citizens. As part of this decision, on 9 November the East German government announced that East Germans would be allowed to cross the border with West Berlin. On hearing this news, thousands of East Berliners flooded the checkpoints in the wall, demanding entry into West Berlin. The border guards let them pass – the Berlin Wall had fallen. Many people started to chip away and dismantle parts of the wall, and ten new border crossings were created by the East German government in the following days. Many people were reunited with friends and relatives thay had been separated from since the wall had been built 30 years before. The opening of the Berlin Wall was the first step towards the reunification of Germany.

The end of the Warsaw Pact

As the Eastern Bloc disintegrated, it became obvious that the Warsaw Pact could not survive. The Pact was an alliance that united the communist states of Eastern Europe against the capitalist states in the West. However, as first Poland, then Hungary and finally East Germany all rejected communism, the Pact no longer served any purpose. Military co-operation ceased in early 1990 and the Warsaw Pact was formally dissolved in July 1991.

examzone
Top tip

Detailed answers will score more highly in the exam. The use of dates is a good way to make your answer more detailed. For example, when writing about the break-up of the Eastern Bloc, try to include the dates on which the different Eastern European countries rejected communism.

Activity

You have been asked to design a museum exhibit on the break-up of the Eastern Bloc. You must produce a proposal for your exhibit. This could be in the form of a poster or a booklet.

Your proposal must include:

- information about how the exhibit would be laid out and how much space should be given to each section of the exhibit
- examples of pictures and documents that could be included in the exhibit (you may need to do some independent research to find these)
- details of the text that you would like to accompany the exhibit.

In your proposal you must explain why you have chosen this layout and defend your choice of pictures and documents.

65

Gorbachev and the end of the Cold War: the fall of the Soviet Union

66

> ### Learning objectives
>
> In this chapter you will learn about:
>
> - the overthrow of President Gorbachev
> - the collapse of the Soviet Union
> - the end of the Cold War.

Soviet reaction to the fall of the Berlin Wall

Gorbachev was undoubtedly the 'darling of the West'. Indeed, British Prime Minister Margaret Thatcher described him as 'a man I can do business with'. He was widely respected for his willingness to reform and the fact that his policies had led to the break-up of Eastern Europe.

At home in Russia, however, Gorbachev was treated with suspicion and cynicism. Leading members of the Communist Party believed that *perestroika* and *glasnost* had weakened communism rather than reviving it. Consequently, on 19 August 1991 a group of senior communist government officials – known as the 'Gang of Eight' – organised a coup which removed Gorbachev from power.

Initially, the coup was successful. Gorbachev, who was away from the capital at the time, was prevented from returning to Moscow. The new government declared a state of emergency, which overturned the freedoms gained during *perestroika* and *glasnost*. The new government's goal was to restore the power of the Soviet Union and secure the future of the communist government.

The new government lasted for three days. Boris Yeltsin, the future president of Russia, played a crucial role in defeating the coup. Yeltsin described the new government as 'illegal' and called on the people of Moscow to resist the new regime.

A group of people sit on top of a tank following the failed coup against Gorbachev, August 1991.

Boris Yeltsin (standing on tank holding papers) prepares to speak to the crowds in Moscow following the failed coup against Gorbachev, August 1991.

Gorbachev's final days as president and the fall of the Soviet Union

On 21 August Gorbachev returned to Moscow and resumed his position as leader of Russia. Immediately following his return, Gorbachev announced that it was still his intention to save Soviet communism. However, the coup had damaged Gorbachev's authority, while it had made Yeltsin a popular hero.

Gorbachev's final attempt to save the Soviet Union was the introduction of a new constitution, which was designed to give the Soviet republics, such as Latvia and the Ukraine, much greater independence. The leaders of these countries, however, wanted full independence, and for this reason the new constitution was never accepted. As a result, Gorbachev officially announced the dissolution of the Soviet Union and his resignation as president on 25 December 1991. The Cold War had ended.

The process of renovating the country and radical changes in the world turned out to be far more complicated than could be expected. However, work of historic significance has been accomplished. The totalitarian system, which deprived the country of an opportunity to become successful and prosperous long ago has been eliminated. Free elections, freedom of the press, religious freedoms, representative organs of power, a multiparty system became a reality; human rights are recognised as the supreme principle.

Extract from Mikhail Gorbachev's resignation speech, December 1991.

The end of the Cold War

American President George Bush had declared that the Cold War was over at the Malta Summit in 1989. However, communism was still undefeated and the coup of August 1991 raised the prospect of another standoff between East and West. The Baltic States (Estonia, Latvia and Lithuania) declared themselves independent in 1990 and this was accepted by the USSR the following year. This led to copy-cat demands within the Soviet Union.

The USSR before its collapse.

The individual states which emerged after the collapse of the USSR.

It seemed that the country was on the brink of collapse. It was the fall of the Soviet Union in December 1991 that finally ended the ideological battle between the capitalist West and the communist East. The dissolution of the Soviet Union also ended superpower conflict, because once the USSR was dissolved, America became the world's only superpower.

Watch out!

Throughout your study of the Cold War you have come across a number of acronyms, such as SALT, SDI, INF, the USSR and NATO. If you only learn the letters, it can be easy to get these confused. Make sure you know what the acronyms stand for.

Activities

You have been commissioned to write a biography of Mikhail Gorbachev, focusing on his role as Russian leader and his contribution to ending the Cold War. You must complete this task in four stages.

1 Write a table of contents with titles for each of the chapters that you are going to write.

2 Write a 20-word summary of the contents of each of the chapters.

3 You have a budget of £2,000 to spend on pictures to illustrate the book. Choose a series of pictures to accompany your chapters. Write a sentence justifying why each picture you have chosen should be in the book. Pictures cost:

- £250 for a black and white image
- £500 for a colour image.

4 Choose a title for the biography that accurately reflects the contents of the book.

Build better answers

Exam question: Explain why relations between the Soviet Union and the USA changed in the years 1979–91. (13 marks)
You may use the following in your answer.
- The end of détente
- The invasion of Afghanistan
You must also include information of your own.
You need to make relevant points, supported by specific examples, with a clear focus on how each factor led to the situation described.

In each level, the number of statements you make will affect the quality of your answer. For example, in level 2, a single developed argument is unlikely to provide as complete an answer as three developed arguments.

■ **A basic answer (level 1)** is correct, but does not have details to support it (for example, *One reason why the relationship between the Soviet Union and the USA changed is because of the end of détente.*).

● **A good answer (level 2)** provides the details as well but does not explain how they caused the process mentioned in the question (for example, *One reason why the relationship between the Soviet Union and the USA changed is because of the end of détente. During détente the superpowers worked together and signed SALT 1, which limited their nuclear capabilities. However, when détente broke down, the US Senate refused to ratify the treaty and President Carter increased defence spending by 5 per cent.*).

▲ **A better answer (level 3)** provides reasons, supports these with detail and explains how they caused the event process mentioned in the question (for example, *One reason why the relationship between the Soviet Union and the USA changed is because of the end of détente. During détente the superpowers worked together and signed SALT 1, which limited their nuclear capabilities. However, when détente broke down, the US Senate refused to ratify the treaty and President Carter increased defence spending by 5 per cent. This shows that the relationship had changed because during détente the USA and the USSR worked together, but after the end of détente they were no longer willing to cooperate. This was important because it allowed the Cold War to spread to outer space with creation of SDI which forced Gorbachev to negotiate with the West.*).

▲ **An excellent answer (level 4)** shows how the reasons are linked and/or reaches a judgement about their relative importance.

Make sure you write accurately – there are 3 extra marks available for spelling, grammar and punctuation in these questions.
Now write another paragraph in answer to this question. Choose one of the points mentioned below, add examples, explain how this factor changed relations between the Soviet Union and the USA in the period stated, and explain how this factor is linked to the factor discussed above and reach a judgement about which of the two factors is most important.
- The invasion of Afghanistan
- The election of President Reagan
- Gorbachev's 'New Thinking'.

Know Zone
Unit 1 – section 6

Exam Zone

In the Unit 1 exam, you will be required to answer questions from two sections. In Section A you will answer three questions: Question 1, Question 2 and Question 3. In Section B you will also answer three questions: Question 4 (where you will have a choice of two questions), Question 5 (where you will have to explain the importance of three events from a choice of four), and Question 6.

You have about 25 minutes to answer the questions in Section A. You might want to spend 3 minutes on Question 1, 7 minutes on Question 2, and 15 minutes on Question 3.

You have about 50 minutes to answer the questions in Section B. You might want to spend 9 minutes on Question 4, 22 minutes on Question 5, and 19 minutes on Question 6.

If you qualify for extra time, remember to include this when you work out your timings.

Build better answers

Question 1

Tip: Question 1 is source-based and will ask you to identify two pieces of information from a source. This question is worth 2 marks. There is one mark available for each piece of information identified. Let's look at an example.

Source A: From a school textbook, written in 2013. It is describing the impact of the Cuban Missile Crisis.
The Cuban Missile Crisis had a series of significant consequences. Kennedy and Khrushchev were both concerned about how close the world had come to nuclear war, and sought measures to reduce the possibility of nuclear conflict. The Limited Test Ban Treaty was introduced as a first step towards controlling nuclear weapons. The Treaty banned the testing of nuclear weapons. In addition both sides agreed to the establishment of a hotline between the US president and the Soviet leader. This was intended to improve communication and create a means for resolving problems.

Study Source A.
Give two reasons from Source A which show that 'the Cuban Missile Crisis had a series of significant consequences' (Source A line 1). (2 marks)

Student answer	Comments
The Limited Test Ban Treaty was introduced to ban the testing of nuclear weapons. This was introduced in 1963, and banned the testing of nuclear weapons in space, the sea and above ground. However, it allowed underground nuclear tests.	The answer provides one reason from Source A. However, it also provides some own knowledge of the topic. As Question 1 does not ask for own knowledge, this response is not as strong as it could be.

Let's rewrite the answer so that it provides two reasons from Source A.

The Limited Test Ban Treaty was introduced to ban the testing of nuclear weapons. In addition, the hotline was created to improve communication between the US President and the Soviet leader.	Two reasons are identified from Source A, thus making it a more complete answer.

examzone

Build better answers

Question 2

Tip: Question 2 will ask you to identify two actions, decisions, causes, factors or changes, and provide some detail about these. This question is worth 4 marks. One mark is awarded for each factor identified (up to a total of two marks), and two additional marks are available for providing detail to support each point. Let's look at an example.

Outline two steps taken by President Truman to contain communism. (4 marks)

Student answer	Comments
One way in which President Truman tried to contain communism was by announcing the Truman Doctrine in 1947. In addition, he also introduced the Marshall Plan in 1947.	The answer provides two steps taken by Truman, However, it does not provide supporting evidence to develop these points, and therefore could be stronger.

Let's rewrite the answer so that it provides two steps taken by Truman to contain communism, but also provides additional detail about these steps. So that you can spot it easily we will put the additional detail in bold.

One way in which President Truman tried to contain communism was by announcing the Truman Doctrine in 1947. **The Truman Doctrine promised American troops and resources to support those countries threatened by communists.** In addition, he also introduced the Marshall Plan in 1947. **This aimed to weaken the appeal of communism by providing economic aid to those countries whose economies had been destroyed by the Second World War.**	Now the answer provides two steps taken by Truman, and provides additional information about each of those steps.

examzone
Build better answers

Question 3

Tip: Question 3 is source-based and will ask you to assess the usefulness of two sources for a specific purpose. This question is worth 10 marks. An excellent answer will consider the usefulness of the information provided by the sources, and an evaluation of their provenance so that the ways in which the sources' nature, origin and purpose affect their usefulness for a specific enquiry can be assessed. It is also important that you use your own knowledge when reaching a judgement.

Source A: A Soviet statement issued in 1961 explaining the reasons for the construction of the Berlin Wall.
The Western powers use Berlin as a centre of rebellious activity against East Germany. Spies are smuggled into East Germany for all kinds of rebellious activity: recruiting more spies, sabotage, provoking disturbances. The government presents all people of East Germany with a proposal that will securely block rebellious activity so that control will be established along the border between West Berlin and East Berlin.

Source B: A table showing the number of people migrating from East Germany to West Germany in the period 1959–1961. The figures are taken from a book about international migration, published in America in1997.

Date:	Number of people migrating from East Germany to West Germany
1959	144,000
1960	199,000
1961	207,000

Study Sources A and B.

How useful are Sources A and B as evidence of the reasons for the construction of the Berlin Wall in August 1961?

Explain your answer, using Sources A and B and your own knowledge. (10 marks)

Student answer

Both sources are very useful. Source A shows that the Soviets were afraid that Western countries were smuggling spies across the border between West Berlin and East Berlin. The source says that these spies are sent to East Berlin with the intention of 'provoking disturbances'. By this they mean that the spies are trying to arrange protests against communism. Source B, on the other hand, is useful because it shows that migration from East Germany to West Germany was increasing. In 1959, migration was 144,000, but by 1961, it had risen to 207,000.

Comments

This answer draws conclusions about the usefulness of the sources based on the information in the sources. A better answer would also consider the provenance of the sources, and would assess the ways in which the nature, origin or purpose of the sources affected their usefulness. In addition, this answer does not make links to the specific enquiry mentioned in the question, and makes no use of own knowledge.

examzone
Build better answers

Let's rewrite the answer so that it considers provenance and the nature of the enquiry, and makes use of own knowledge.

Both sources are very useful as evidence of the reasons for the construction of the Berlin Wall in August 1961. Source A shows that the Soviets were afraid that Western countries were smuggling spies across the border between West Berlin and East Berlin. The source says that these spies are sent to East Berlin with the intention of 'provoking disturbances'. By this they mean that the spies are trying to arrange protests against communism. In this sense, the source is useful because it suggests that the Berlin Wall was constructed to prevent spies from entering East Berlin. Source B, on the other hand, is useful because it shows that migration from East Germany to West Germany was increasing. In 1959, migration was 144,000, but by 1961, it had risen to 207,000. Many refugees entered West Germany via West Berlin as the border in Berlin was easy to cross. Also, many of the refugees were skilled workers, who played an important economic role in East Germany. Therefore, the source is useful because it tells us that the Wall was constructed in order to solve the refugee crisis. However, there are limitations to the usefulness of both sources. Source A provides a Soviet explanation of the reasons for the construction of the Berlin Wall. The Soviets would not want to admit that thousands of people were leaving East Germany for a better life in West Germany, and therefore the source presents a reason that does not expose the weaknesses of the communist system. Source B is from a book published after the end of the Cold War and so there is no obvious reason for the figures to have been distorted. However, the usefulness of Source B is limited because many people escaped from East Germany secretly, and therefore the statistics will be estimates. In reality, the figures could be much higher or much lower. Overall, therefore, the sources provide useful information, about the reasons for the construction of the Berlin Wall, but the reliability and accuracy of that information is more limited.

This answer is a strong one because it draws conclusions about the usefulness of the sources based on the information in the sources and the provenance of the sources. In addition, it makes use of own knowledge and links its conclusions to the specific enquiry mentioned in the question.

Note that the comments about the reliability of the sources focus on their reliability for the purpose stated in the question. Rather than saying 'Source A is unreliable because it is from a Soviet perspective,' the answer explains how the perspective of the source may alter its account of why the Berlin Wall was constructed.

Question 4

Question 4 will ask you to describe the key features of a major policy or an event. This question is worth 6 marks.
One mark is awarded for each simple statement, with an additional three marks available for supporting evidence.
Make sure that when you describe the key features, you don't just tell the story: think about the information and organise it as if you were putting it under headings.

Describe the key features of the arms race. (6 marks)

Student answer

One key feature of the arms race was the competition between the superpowers to create more and more powerful nuclear weapons. At first, the United States was ahead in the race as it was the first country to make atomic bombs. These were 'Fat Man', and 'Little Boy' which were dropped on Japan at the end of the Second World War. By 1949, the USSR had caught up and tested its own atomic bomb. Next were hydrogen bombs, which were even more powerful. Once again, America was first but the USSR soon caught up with its first hydrogen bomb, which it called 'Layercake'.

Comments

This is a very detailed account of one key feature of the arms race. However, in order to produce a more complete answer you need to make two or three developed points about key features.

examzone

Build better answers

Let's rewrite the answer to mention the competition between the superpowers but also to explain two more key features. So that you can spot them easily we will put the key features in bold.

> **One key feature of the arms race was the competition between the superpowers to create more nuclear weapons.** The USA was the first country to use atomic bombs in 1945. By 1949, the USSR had caught up and tested its own atomic bomb. **Another key feature of the arms race was that it preserved peace in Europe.** The USSR had three million troops in Eastern Germany and could easily have defeated Western Germany. However, the USA put nuclear missiles in Western Europe and this prevented any Soviet invasion. **A third key feature of the arms race was that it led to better military technology.** The first nuclear bombs were very powerful, but the second generation of nuclear bombs were hydrogen bombs, such as the Russian 'Layercake', which were even more deadly.

This answer makes three points and backs them up with examples to provide a very strong response.

Question 5

Question 5 asks you to explain the importance of three out of four events listed in the question. 5 marks are available for each part of the question, up to a total of 15 marks. Do not just describe each event. Instead, focus on explaining, with supporting evidence, why the event was important. Below is an example of an answer to one part of the question. Don't forget that in the exam, you will have to explain the importance of three events, not just one.

Explain the importance of the following in international relations:

• The Soviet invasion of Afghanistan, 1979 (5 marks)

Student answer

In 1979, Brezhnev ordered the Soviet invasion of Afghanistan with the aim of consolidating a communist regime in Afghanistan. It was an important event because it angered the USA and led to the end of détente.

Comments

This answer describes the event and states why the event was important. However, it does not explain the importance of the event, and it does not provide detailed evidence to support the argument.

Let's rewrite the answer so that it provides greater explanation and supporting evidence.

> The Soviet invasion of Afghanistan in 1979 was extremely important as it worsened relations between the USSR and the USA and led to the end of détente. The US government interpreted the invasion as an attempt by the USSR to expand their territory in the oil-rich Middle East. Consequently, President Carter took steps to try to force Soviet troops out of Afghanistan. In addition, he withdrew his support for the SALT 2 Treaty, which would have reduced the number of nuclear weapons held by each superpower. Finally, Carter led a boycott of the 1980 Moscow Olympics. As a result, superpower relations deteriorated, spelling the end of détente.

This answer does not describe the event, but instead explains the importance of the event, and makes use of detailed evidence to support its explanation. For this reason, it is a strong answer.

Question 6

Question 6 requires extended writing. This question will ask you to use your own knowledge to explain why something happened. You should try to find three or four reasons and explain how they led to the outcome stated in the question. It is important that you provide reasons beyond those that are suggested in the question. An excellent answer will not only explain three or four reasons, but will also draw links between these reasons, and explain which reason was most important. There are 13 marks available for your answer, with an additional 3 marks awarded for spelling, punctuation and grammar.

Explain why relations between the Soviet Union and the USA changed in 1962. (13 marks)
You may use the following in your answer.
- The Soviet Union placed missiles on Cuba
- Kennedy's reaction to the placement of missiles on Cuba.
You must also include information of your own.

Student answer	Comments
In 1962, relations between the Soviet Union and the USA changed because the Soviet Union placed missiles on Cuba. Cuba was only 90 miles from the coast of America and because of this Americans felt very threatened by the arrival of Russian nuclear weapons, which were capable of destroying whole American cities. This made the relationship worse because the Americans thought that this was a very aggressive thing to do.	This answer is good because it provides a reason why relations between the Soviet Union and the USA changed in 1962, it explains how this reason changed the relationship, and it provides relevant own knowledge to support the explanation. However, as it provides only one reason, it is not a complete answer.

Let's rewrite the answer to provide two more reasons, with examples and explanation. So that you can spot them easily, we have put the reasons in bold.

In 1962, the relationship between the Soviet Union and the USA changed a great deal. At first it got much worse. However, by the end of the year, the relationship had improved. **The first reason for the change was that the Soviet Union placed missiles on Cuba.** Cuba was only 90 miles from the coast of America and because of this Americans felt very threatened by the arrival of Russian nuclear weapons, which were capable of destroying whole American cities. This made the relationship worse because the Americans thought that this was a very aggressive thing to do. **This led to the second reason for the change, Kennedy's first reaction to the missiles on Cuba.** Kennedy publicly demanded that the USSR remove its weapons and ordered a naval blockade of Cuba. In September 1962, 114 Soviet ships had set sail for Cuba carrying nuclear warheads and long-range missiles. The blockade was designed to prevent these ships from reaching Cuba. This made the relationship even worse because it looked like both sides were heading for a nuclear war, despite the fact that neither side wanted this. **Thirdly, in order to avoid nuclear war, Kennedy sent his brother to do a deal with the USSR.** In the deal, the USSR agreed to remove the missiles from Cuba, and the USA agreed to remove the missiles that it had in Turkey. This made the relationship better because the two sides agreed a private deal which stopped a nuclear war. Overall, the most important factor that changed the relationship between the USA and the USSR in 1962 was Khrushchev's decision to place missiles on Cuba because without this, none of the other changes would have happened.	This answer is an improvement on the previous answer because it makes three points and links these points together, showing how each point led to the next. What makes it a strong answer is that it also prioritises the factors, explaining which is the most important.
Also make sure you write accurately – there are 3 extra marks available for spelling, grammar and punctuation in these questions. It is worthwhile planning in some time to check the accuracy of your writing once you have completed your answer.

Know Zone

In this zone, you'll find some useful suggestions about how to structure your revision, and checklists to help you test your learning for each of the main topics. You might want to skim-read this before you start your revision planning, as it will help you think about how best to revise the content.

Revision techniques

Remember that different people learn in different ways – some remember visually and therefore might want to think about using diagrams and other drawings for their revision, whereas others remember better through sound or through writing things out. Think about what works best for you by trying out some of the techniques below.

- **Summaries**: writing a summary of the information in a chapter can be a useful way of making sure you've understood it. But don't just copy it all out. Try to reduce each paragraph to a couple of sentences. Then try to reduce the couple of sentences to a few words!

- **Concept maps**: if you're a visual learner, you may find it easier to take in information by representing it visually. Draw concept maps or other diagrams. These are particularly good at showing links. For example, you could create a concept map which shows the reasons for the end of the Cold War, with arrows pointing to such things as 'the role of Gorbachev', 'the role of Reagan' etc.

- **Mnemonics**: this is when you take the first letter of a series of words you want to remember and then make a new word or sentence.

- **Index cards**: write important events and people on index cards then test yourself on why they were important.

- **Timelines**: create a large, visual timeline and annotate it in colour.

- **Quizzes**: let's face it, learning stuff can be dull. Why not make a quiz out of it? Set a friend 20 questions to answer. Make up multiple-choice questions. You might even make up your own exam-style questions and see if your friend can answer them!

And then when you are ready:

- practice questions – go back through the sample exam-style questions in this book to see if you can answer them (without cheating!)

- try writing out some of your answers in timed conditions so that you're used to the amount of time you'll have to answer each type of question in the exam.

If you are sitting your exams from 2014 onwards, you will be sitting all your exams together at the end of your course. Make sure you know in which order you are sitting the exams, and prepare for each accordingly – check with your teacher if you're not sure. They are likely to be about a week apart, so make sure you allow plenty of revision time for each before your first exam.

Know Zone Unit 1 Key Topic 1

You should know about the following things. If you can't remember any of them, just look at the page number and re-read that chapter.

❏ The difference between communism and capitalism **(pages 6–9)**

❏ The three key meetings of the Grand Alliance **(pages 6–9)**

❏ The difficult relationship between Russia and America before the Cold War began **(pages 6–9)**

❏ The breakdown of trust between Russia and America **(pages 10–11)**

❏ How Russia and America viewed each other in 1946 **(pages 10–11)**

❏ The key features of the Truman Doctrine and Marshall Aid **(pages 12–13)**

❏ America's reasons for offering Marshall Aid **(pages 12–13)**

❏ Stalin's control of the satellite states **(pages 14–16)**

❏ Why Stalin established Cominform and Comecon **(pages 16–17)**

❏ How the 'spheres of influence' became 'two camps' **(pages 14–17)**

❏ The division of Germany into East and West **(pages 18–19)**

❏ The impact of the Berlin Blockade **(pages 18–23)**

❏ The formation of NATO and the arms race **(pages 20–21)**

❏ The effect of Soviet rule on Hungary **(pages 22–25)**

❏ The causes and consequences of 'de-Stalinisation' **(pages 22–25)**

❏ The impact of the Hungarian revolt of 1956 **(pages 22–25)**

Key events

Do you know why these events are important? If not, go back to the page and look them up!

1941 Grand Alliance created **(page 6)**

1943 Teheran Conference **(page 6)**

1945 Yalta Conference **(page 7)**

1945 Potsdam Conference **(page 8)**

1946 Churchill's 'Iron Curtain' speech **(page 10)**

1946 Long Telegram sent **(page 10)**

1946 Novikov's Telegram sent **(page 10)**

1947 Truman Doctrine announced **(page 12)**

1947 Marshall Plan announced **(page 12)**

1947 Cominform created **(page 16)**

1948 Paris Conference **(page 17)**

1948–9 Berlin Blockade **(page 19)**

1949 Comecon created **(page 17)**

1949 West Germany and East Germany created **(page 19)**

1949 Formation of NATO **(page 20)**

1955 Warsaw Pact established **(page 20)**

1956 Khrushchev's 'Secret Speech' **(page 22)**

1956 Soviet invasion of Hungary **(page 23)**

Key people

Do you know why these people are important?

Franklin D. Roosevelt	Matyas Rakosi
Winston Churchill	Nikita Khrushchev
Joseph Stalin	Dwight D. Eisenhower
Harry S. Truman	Janos Kadar

Exam Zone

Know Zone Unit 1 Key Topic 2

You should know about the following things. If you can't remember any of them, just look at the page number and re-read that chapter.

78

- ❏ The refugee problem facing the East German government **(page 27)**
- ❏ Khrushchev's response to this crisis **(page 27)**
- ❏ The failure of negotiations with Khrushchev over the future of Berlin **(pages 28–29)**
- ❏ Khrushchev's ultimatum and Kennedy's preparation for war **(pages 28–29)**
- ❏ The reasons for the creation of the Berlin Wall **(pages 30–31)**
- ❏ Kennedy's response to the building of the Berlin Wall **(pages 30–31)**
- ❏ The development of the arms race between 1945 and 1961 **(pages 32–35)**
- ❏ The effects of Cuba's revolution **(pages 32–35)**
- ❏ Khrushchev's decision to build missile bases on Cuba **(pages 32–35)**
- ❏ How America learned of Khrushchev's plan **(pages 36–37)**
- ❏ The 'hawks and the doves' **(page 37)**
- ❏ The events of the 'Thirteen Days' **(pages 36–37)**
- ❏ The immediate consequences of the Cuban Missile Crisis, including the creation of the 'hotline', the Test Ban Treaty and détente **(page 38)**
- ❏ The long-term consequences of the Cuban Missile Crisis, including the doctrine of Mutually Assured Destruction (MAD) and the French decision to leave NATO **(page 39)**
- ❏ Czechoslovakian opposition to Soviet control **(pages 40–41)**
- ❏ Dubcek's attitude to communism **(pages 40–41)**
- ❏ The events of the 'Prague Spring' **(pages 40–41)**
- ❏ The re-establishment of Soviet control in Czechoslovakia **(pages 42–43)**
- ❏ The Brezhnev Doctrine **(page 42)**
- ❏ The Soviet invasion of Czechoslovakia **(pages 42–43)**
- ❏ America's reaction to the Soviet invasion of Czechoslovakia **(page 44)**
- ❏ The divisions in European communism created by the invasion **(page 44)**

Key events

Do you know why these events are important? If not, go back to the page and look them up!

1957 Russian scientists launch Sputnik 1 **(page 34)**

1959 Geneva Summit **(page 28)**

1960 Paris Conference **(page 28)**

1961 Vienna Conference **(page 28)**

1961 East German troops erect a barbed wire fence around West Berlin **(page 30)**

1961 Bay of Pigs invasion **(page 34)**

1962 Premier Khrushchev sends nuclear missiles to Cuba **(page 35)**

1962 Cuban Missile Crisis **(page 36)**

1963 President Kennedy visits Berlin **(page 31)**

1963 'Hotline' between Washington and Moscow created **(page 38)**

1963 Limited Test Ban Treaty **(page 38)**

1968 'Prague Spring' **(page 41)**

1968 Soviet invasion of Czechoslovakia **(page 42)**

Key people

Do you know why these people are important?

John F. Kennedy   Dwight D. Eisenhower   Leonid Brezhnev   Josip Broz Tito

Nikita Khrushchev   Alexander Dubcek   Lyndon B. Johnson

You should know about the following things. If you can't remember any of the following things just look at the page number and re-read that chapter.

- ❑ The treaties in 1967 and 1968 which began détente **(page 47)**
- ❑ The SALT 1 Treaty, the Helsinki Conference and the Apollo–Soyuz mission **(pages 47–49)**
- ❑ The Kabul Revolution **(pages 50–51)**
- ❑ The establishment of a communist regime in Afghanistan **(pages 50–51)**
- ❑ The reasons for the Soviet invasion of Afghanistan **(pages 50–51)**
- ❑ President Carter's immediate reaction to the invasion of Afghanistan **(pages 52–53)**
- ❑ The failure of the SALT 2 Treaty **(page 53)**
- ❑ The American boycott of the Moscow Olympic Games **(page 53)**
- ❑ What is meant by the Second Cold War **(pages 54–55)**
- ❑ President Reagan's attitude to the Cold War **(pages 54–55)**
- ❑ The 'Evil Empire' speech **(pages 54–55)**
- ❑ Reagan's vision of SDI **(pages 56–57)**
- ❑ The problems created by SDI **(pages 56–57)**
- ❑ The shift in the arms race **(pages 56–57)**
- ❑ Gorbachev's vision for communism **(pages 58–59)**
- ❑ Gorbachev's relationship with the West **(page 58)**
- ❑ Gorbachev's 'new thinking' **(page 59)**
- ❑ The strengths and weaknesses of the superpowers in 1985 **(pages 60–63)**
- ❑ Three summits and the INF Treaty **(pages 60–63)**
- ❑ The reasons for the changing relationship between the USA and the USSR **(pages 60–63)**
- ❑ Gorbachev's attitude to Eastern Europe **(pages 64–65)**
- ❑ The break-up of the Eastern Bloc **(pages 64–65)**
- ❑ The fall of the Berlin Wall and the end of the Warsaw Pact **(page 65)**
- ❑ The overthrow of President Gorbachev **(pages 66–67)**
- ❑ Gorbachev's final days in office and the fall of the Soviet Union **(pages 66–69)**
- ❑ The end of the Cold War **(pages 68–69)**

1967 Outer Space Treaty **(page 46)**

1968 Nuclear Non-proliferation Treaty **(page 47)**

1972 SALT 1 **(page 47)**

1975 Helsinki Conference **(page 48–49)**

1975 Apollo–Soyuz mission **(page 48)**

1978 Kabul Revolution **(page 50)**

1979 Soviet invasion of Afghanistan **(page 50)**

1980 Moscow Olympic Games **(page 52)**

1983 Reagan's 'Evil Empire' speech **(page 53)**

1983 Reagan proposes SDI **(page 56)**

1984 Los Angeles Olympic Games **(page 52)**

1985 Geneva Summit **(page 60)**

1986 Chernobyl disaster **(page 58)**

1986 Reykjavik Summit **(page 60)**

1987 INF Treaty **(page 61)**

1989 Communist government falls in Poland, Hungary and Czechoslovakia **(page 64)**

1989 Fall of the Berlin Wall **(page 65)**

1991 Warsaw Pact dissolved **(page 65)**

1991 'Gang of Eight' removes Gorbachev from power **(page 66)**

1991 Gorbachev resigns and announces the fall of the Soviet Union **(page 67)**

Key people

Do you know why these people are important?

Ronald Reagan   Jimmy Carter
Mikhail Gorbachev   Boris Yeltsin
Leonid Brezhnev

Don't Panic Zone

As the day of the exam gets closer, many students tend to go into panic mode, either working long hours without really giving their brain a chance to absorb information, or giving up and staring blankly at the wall.

Look over your revision notes and go through the checklists to remind yourself of the main areas you need to know about. Don't try to cram in too much new information at the last minute and don't stay up late revising – you'll do better if you get a good night's sleep.

Exam Zone

You will have 1 hour and 15 minutes in the examination. There will be two sections in the Unit 1 exam paper. In Section A you will answer three questions: Question 1, Question 2 and Question 3. In Section B you will also answer three questions: Question 4 (where you will have a choice of two questions), Question 5 (where you will have to explain the importance of three events from a choice of four), and Question 6.

You have about 25 minutes to answer the questions in Section A. You might want to spend 3 minutes on Question 1, 7 minutes on Question 2, and 15 minutes on Question 3.

You have about 50 minutes to answer the questions in Section B. You might want to spend 9 minutes on Question 4, 22 minutes on Question 5, and 19 minutes on Question 6.

If you qualify for extra time, remember to include this when you work out your timings.

Question 1 is worth 2 marks.

Question 1 is source-based and will ask you to identify two pieces of information from a source. There is one mark available for each piece of information identified.

Page 72 has an example of this type of question.

Question 2 is worth 4 marks.

Question 2 will ask you to identify two actions, decisions, causes, factors or changes, and provide some detail about these. One mark is awarded for each factor identified (up to a total of two marks), and two additional marks are available for providing detail to support each point.

Page 73 has an example of this type of question.

Question 3 is worth 10 marks.

Question 3 is source-based and will ask you to assess the usefulness of two sources for a specific purpose. When reaching a judgement about usefulness, you need to consider the information provided by the source, the provenance of the source, and the purpose stated in the question. It is also important that use your own knowledge when reaching a judgement.

Page 74 has an example of this type of question.

Question 4 is worth 6 marks.

Question 4 will ask you to describe the key features of a major policy or an event. One mark is awarded for each simple statement, with an additional three marks available for supporting evidence. Make sure that when you describe the key features, you don't just tell the story: think about the information and organise it as if you were putting it under headings.

Page 75 has an example of this type of question.

Question 5 is worth 15 marks.

Question 5 asks you to explain the importance of three out of four events listed in the question. 5 marks are available for each part of the question, up to a total of 15 marks – you will not gain extra marks for describing the importance of all four events! Do not just describe each event. Instead, focus on explaining, with supporting evidence, why the event was important.

Page 76 has an example of this type of question.

Question 6 is worth 13 marks, with an additional 3 marks available for spelling, punctuation and grammar.

Question 6 will ask you to use your own knowledge to explain why something happened. The question will list two possible reasons. You should make use of these reasons, but also provide one or two additional reasons from your own knowledge. An excellent answer will not only explain three or four reasons, but will also draw links between these reasons, and explain which reason was most important.

Page 77 has an example of this type of question.

Meet the exam paper

In this exam you will write all of your answers in the spaces provided on the exam paper. It's important that you use a black pen and that you indicate clearly which questions you have answered where a choice is provided – instructions will be given on the paper. Try to make your handwriting as legible as possible.

This diagram shows the front cover and two pages from a sample exam paper. These instructions, information and advice will always appear on the front of the paper. It is worth reading it carefully now as well as in the exam. Check you understand it and ask your teacher about anything you are not sure of.

If possible, ask your teacher to show you an example of a past paper before your exam so that you know what to expect before you go in.

Print your surname here, and your other names afterwards. This is an additional safeguard to ensure that the exam board awards the marks to the right candidate.

Here you fill in the school's exam number.

The Unit 1 exam lasts 1 hour 15 minutes. Plan your time accordingly.

Make sure that you understand exactly which questions you should attempt.

Here you fill in your personal exam number. Take care to write it accurately.

In this box, the examiner will write the total marks you have achieved in the exam paper.

Don't feel that you have to fill the answer space provided. Everybody's handwriting varies, so a long answer from you may take up as much space as a short answer from someone else.

Write your name here

Surname

Other names

**Pearson
Edexcel GCSE**

Centre Number

Candidate Number

History A (The Making of the Modern World)
Unit 1: International Relations
The Era of the Cold War, 1943–91

Sample Assessment Material for 2013
Time: 1 hour 15 minutes

Paper Reference
5HA01/01

You do not need any other materials.

Total Marks

Instructions

- Use **black** ink or ball-point pen.
- **Fill in the boxes** at the top of this page with your name, centre number and candidate number.
- Answer **ALL** questions in **Section A**. In **Section B** answer **EITHER** Question 4(a) **OR** 4(b) and then Question 5 **and** Question 6.
- Answer the questions in the spaces provided – there may be more space than you need.

Information

- The total mark for this paper is 53.
- The marks for **each** question are shown in brackets – use this as a guide as to how much time to spend on each question.
- Questions labelled with an **asterisk** (*) are ones where the quality of your written communication will be assessed
- The marks available for spelling, punctuation and grammar are clearly indicated.

Advice

- Read each question carefully before you start to answer it.
- Keep an eye on the time.
- Check your answers if you have time at the end.

S44045A

PEARSON

Edexcel GCSE in History A   Sample Assessment Materials   © Pearson Education Ltd 2013

Section A

Answer Question 1, Question 2 and Question 3.

Question 1.

Study Source A.

Source A: From a school textbook, written in 2008. It is describing the impact of the Soviet invasion of Afghanistan in 1979.

> The Soviet Union completely miscalculated the impact that its actions would have on the West. The invasion was seen in the West as evidence of Soviet expansion. President Carter stated that the invasion might pose the most serious threat to world peace since World War Two. He took steps to try to persuade the Soviet Union to remove its troops. After 1981, the USA took a more aggressive approach towards the Soviet Union and began to find ways to support the Mujahedin in its fight against Soviet troops in Afghanistan.

1   Give **two** reasons from Source A which show that 'the Soviet Union completely miscalculated the impact that its actions would have on the West' (Source A lines 1–2).
(2)

1 ....

2 ....

(Total for Question 1 = 2 marks)

Edexcel GCSE in History A   Sample Assessment Materials   © Pearson Education Ltd 2013

Pay attention to words in bold, especially numbers. Make sure you give the number of features the question asks for.

Check that you are answering the right number of questions in the right section. In Unit 1 you should answer **ALL** questions in Section A.

In Section B answer **EITHER** Question 4(a) OR 4(b) and then **BOTH** Question 5 and Question 6.

The number of marks available for each question is given on the right.

Section B

Answer EITHER Question 4(a) OR Question 4(b).

EITHER

4   (a) Describe the key features of the 'refugee problem' in Berlin in the years 1958–61.
(6)

OR

4   (b) Describe the key features of the Intermediate-range Nuclear Forces (INF) Treaty signed December 1987.
(6)

Indicate which question you are answering by marking a cross in the box ☒. If you change your mind, put a line through the box ☒ and then indicate your new question with a cross ☒.

Chosen Question Number: Question 4(a) ☐   Question 4(b) ☐

Edexcel GCSE in History A   Sample Assessment Materials   © Pearson Education Ltd 2013

Pay careful attention to which sub-questions and question parts you are required to answer. Mark the relevant box as instructed on the exam paper.

Read dates in questions carefully.

Zone Out

This section provides answers to the most common questions students have about what happens after they complete their exams. For more information, visit www.examzone.co.uk.

When will my results be published?

Results for GCSE examinations are issued on the third Thursday in August.

Can I get my results online?

Visit www.resultsplusdirect.co.uk, where you will find detailed student results information including the 'Edexcel Gradeometer' which demonstrates how close you were to the nearest grade boundary.

I haven't done as well as I expected. What can I do now?

First of all, talk to your teacher. After all the teaching that you have had, and the tests and internal examinations you have done, he/she is the person who best knows what grade you are capable of achieving. Take your results slip to your subject teacher, and go through the information on it in detail. If you both think that there is something wrong with the result, the school or college can apply to see your completed examination paper and then, if necessary, ask for a re-mark immediately.

Can I have a re-mark of my examination paper?

Yes, this is possible, but remember only your school or college can apply for a re-mark, not you or your parents/carers. First of all you should consider carefully whether or not to ask your school or college to make a request for a re-mark. It is worth knowing that very few re-marks result in a change to a grade, simply because a re-mark request has shown that the original marking was accurate. Check the closing date for re-marking requests with your Examinations Officer.

Bear in mind that there is no guarantee that your grades will go up if your papers are re-marked. The original mark can be confirmed or lowered, as well as raised, as a result of a re-mark.

Glossary

Term	Definition
alliance	A formal agreement between countries.
arms race	When countries compete to have the most effective armed forces.
atomic bomb	A highly destructive nuclear weapon.
B52 bomber	A heavy-duty military aircraft capable of crossing large distances and carrying heavy loads.
ballistic nuclear missiles	Nuclear missiles capable of being launched from one continent and hitting targets in another.
Big Three	Roosevelt (United States), Stalin (Soviet Union) and Churchill (Britain) – the original leaders of the Grand Alliance.
blockade	An attempt to prevent resources reaching their destination.
boycott	To refuse to take part in something.
CIA	Central Intelligence Agency – an American organisation designed to monitor foreign governments.
doctrine	A statement of ideas.
Eastern Bloc	The European countries within the Soviet sphere of influence.
economic sanction	A restriction on trade with another country.
fallout shelters	Buildings designed to protect people in the event of a nuclear attack.
Grand Alliance	The military pact between the USA, the USSR and Great Britain, in order to defeat Nazi Germany during the Second World War.
nuclear holocaust	The virtual destruction of the human race by nuclear weapons.
pact	An agreement.
propaganda	Information that is deliberately designed to win political support
refugee	Someone fleeing from bad conditions.
retaliation	An attempt to pay someone back for a wrongdoing.
space race	A period from the late 1950s to the early 1970s during which the USA and the USSR competed to achieve 'firsts' in space.
summit	A high-level meeting between government representatives.
ultimatum	A demand

Published by Pearson Education Limited, Edinburgh Gate, Harlow, Essex, CM20 2JE.
www.pearsonschoolsandfecolleges.co.uk

Copies of official specifications for all Edexcel qualifications may be found on the Edexcel website: www.edexcel.com

Text © Pearson Education Limited 2013
Typeset by HL Studios, Long Hanborough, Oxford
Illustrated by Peter Bull Studio
Cover photo/illustration © Front: **Corbis**: Bettmann

The rights of Robin Bunce, Laura Gallagher and Nigel Kelly to be identified as authors of this work have been asserted by them in accordance with the Copyright, Designs and Patents Act 1988.

First published 2013

16 15 14
10 9 8 7 6 5 4 3

British Library Cataloguing in Publication Data
A catalogue record for this book is available from the British Library

ISBN 978 1 446 90678 1

Printed in Italy by Lego S.p.A

Acknowledgements
The author and publisher would like to thank the following individuals and organisations for permission to reproduce photographs: (Key: b-bottom; c-centre; l-left; r-right; t-top)

Corbis: 20, 26, 20, 26, Bettmann 7, 11, 24 (Khruschev), 45bc, 48, 62, Bettmann 7, 11, 24 (Khruschev), 45bc, 48, 62, Bettmann 7, 11, 24 (Khruschev), 45bc, 48, 62, Bettmann 7, 11, 24 (Khruschev), 45bc, 48, 62, Bettmann 7, 11, 24 (Khruschev), 45bc, 48, 62, Bettmann 7, 11, 24 (Khruschev), 45bc, 48, 62, epa / Libor Hajsky 43, Hulton-Deutsch Collection 24 (Kadar), Wally McNamee 46, Reuters 58, Sygma / J. L. Atlan 32, Peter Turnley 65; **Getty Images**: Hulton Archive 19, 24 (Eisenhower), 37, Hulton Archive 19, 24 (Eisenhower), 37, Time & Life Pictures 22, 24 (Revolutionary), Time & Life Pictures 22, 24 (Revolutionary), Universal Images Group 2; **Mirrorpix**: 4; **nisyndication.com**: 55; **Photoshot Holdings Limited**: UPPA 44; **Press Association Images**: AP 28, 67, AP 28, 67; **Rex Features**: Arthur Grace 52, Everett Collection / CSU Archives 45bl, Poderni-White 66, Sipa Press 31; **RIA Novosti Photo Library**: 33; **Solo Syndication / Associated Newspapers Ltd**: Illingworth, Leslie Gilbert, Daily Mail, 14 February 1949, The National Library of Wales 21b, Illingworth, Leslie Gilbert, Daily Mail, 20 April 1949, The National Library of Wales 21t, Illingworth, Leslie Glibert, 30 June 1948, The National Library of Wales 13; **The Herb Block Foundation**: 38; **TopFoto**: RIA Novosti 45br, Topham Picturepoint 30

All other images © Pearson Education

We are grateful to the following for permission to reproduce copyright material:

Source A, page 10 from Winston Churchill Churchill's 'Iron Curtain' speech, March 1946.; Source A, page 70 from *A World Divided: Superpower Relations, 1944-90 (Hodder, 2013)* p.44 (Les Barker, Robin Bunce and Laura Gallagher); Extract on page 59 adapted from *The Rise and Fall of the Soviet Empire, 1999*. ISBN-13: 978-0006388180 *Harper Collins 20 Aug 2010* (Dimitri Volkogonov), reprinted by permission of HarperCollins Publishers Ltd copyright 2010.

Every effort has been made to contact copyright holders of material reproduced in this book. Any omissions will be rectified in subsequent printings if notice is given to the publishers.